RESTORED: OUR STORY

STEVE REEVES

COLLEGE PRESS PUBLISHING COMPANY

Joplin, Missouri

RESTORED! OUR STORY
Copyright 2018
ISBN: 978-0-89900-556-0
College Press Publishing Co
Order toll-free 800-289-3300
On the web at www.collegepress.com

Library of Congress Cataloging-in-Publication Data

DEDICATION

To my ministry and lifelong marriage partner of over 40 years, Kristen, who has modeled what a Restored Life looks like to the congregations we've served and the family we've raised.

CONTENTS

Forward by Bob Russell 7

Introduction. 9

Chapter 1 – Restored Identity 11

Chapter 2 – Restored Unity 25

Chapter 3 – Restored Plan 39

Chapter 4 – Restored Life 51

Chapter 5 – Restored Wisdom. 67

Chapter 6 – Restored Families. 81

Chapter 7 – Restored Respect 95

Chapter 8 – Restored Victory 109

Addendum – Pastoral Succession 121

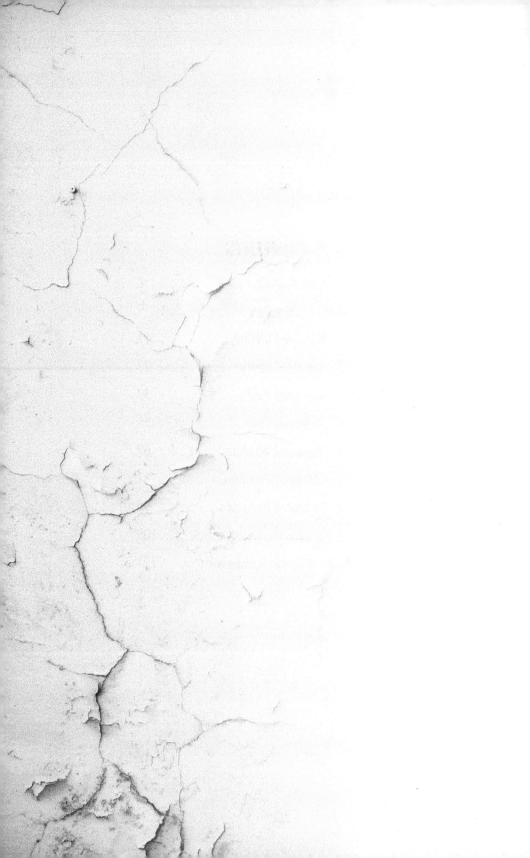

FOREWORD
by BOB RUSSELL

I met Steve Reeves over 40 years ago when he was a minister in Mount Washington, Ohio, just outside Cincinnati. He was a young, handsome preacher who was committed to sharing the Gospel message and caring for his people. A great shepherd of the flock, Steve later did an outstanding job growing the Connection Pointe Church in Indianapolis, Indiana to several thousand believers attending each week. His church loved him because it was obvious that he loved them.

In recounting this history, the Connection Pointe website states matter-of-factly: "In 1986 Pastor Steve Reeves became the 35th senior pastor. Under his leadership, the church experienced consistent growth from a congregation of 250 to over 4000 today." Actually I don't know how you can write that sentence without adding an exclamation point or two at the end. What a marvelous, God-honoring career!! And if there was a book about this history and how it came to be, I would buy that book, read it, study it and then put it into action. I would also recommend everyone read it. The good news is that such a book exists, you have it in your hands right now and the only question is what are you going to do after you read it.

In the book you are about to read Steve makes it easy for us by establishing a standard format in each chapter: "Restoring Me," "Restoring the Church" and "Action Steps" or practical things you can do to translate Biblical concepts into reality. In the seven chapters, Steve elaborates on the seven priorities of Jesus: The Church, Transforming the Neighborhood,

Evangelism, Discipleship, Leadership, The Hurting and Commitment---each is an important subject if you are planning, praying, and expecting to grow from a handful of believers into a healthy church that transforms thousands of lives.

Of the priorities of Jesus, the chapter on evangelism really resonated with me.

You can tell it motivated Steve as well, and I would conclude that an unrelenting passion for outreach is the primary factor that distinguishes all growing churches in America today. It certainly served congregations well at Connection Pointe in Indianapolis, Indiana and at Southeast Christian Church in Louisville, Kentucky, the church I served for 40 years.

Regarding evangelism Steve wrote: "God's plan for saving the world – His only plan for the world - is for the Church, manifested in the individual believers of which it is comprised, to cast a bright light into the darkness and share the Gospel with those who are yet far off, separated from a God who desperately wants all people to come to a knowledge of His truth, love, and grace." True to his word, Steve shares numerous, helpful, practical initiatives in this chapter that will enable you and your church to enrich your outreach programs.

Saving the best for last, Steve closes his book with a brief, but insightful, addendum on the topic of church succession. It's my observation, until relatively recently, most of our churches have not done a good job of transitioning from one senior pastor to another. As a result the church often experiences an avoidable decline in both spirit and involvement. Many churches are now making an effort to do better in this regard and Steve's practical insights at the end of his book will prove very helpful in succession planning.

I am encouraged that while not as young as when I first met Steve he is still as energetic and as committed to church growth as ever. After you have read his book you will see why this is true and, perhaps, see how God can use you to grow your church by sharing the Gospel message and caring for your people.

BOB RUSSELL
Retired Senior Minister
Southeast Christian Church

INTRODUCTION

I am honored that you have chosen to pick up this book and go on a journey with me in a process I've entitled, *"Restored: Our Story."*

We will hit the high points, from the New Testament letter of Ephesians, that God has used to restore each of us individually, and our churches, independently. In each chapter we will discuss "Restoring Me" ..."Restoring the Church" … "ACTION STEPS FOR OUR STORY."

In my new season of post-retirement, after forty years of local pastoral ministry, I am currently serving as an advisor with The Center for Church Leadership, located in Cincinnati, Ohio. I am indebted to Tim Wallingford and Jeffrey Derico for the material at the end of chapters 1-7 on "The Seven Priorities of Jesus."

This book is a celebration of what it means to be restored to the Lord and His Church! Since Jesus is the only Head of the Church, it is most appropriate to consider "The Seven Priorities of Jesus," as we and our churches take ACTION STEPS in the ongoing process of being Restored!

A work of restoration in progress,
STEVEN T. REEVES

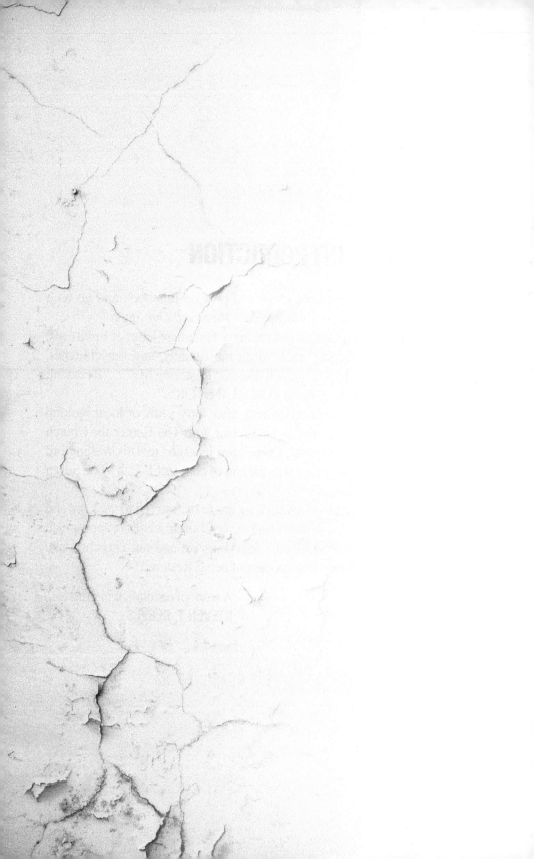

CHAPTER ONE
RESTORED IDENTITY

It was Friday night at church camp, just outside of Clovis, New Mexico. I was 9 years old and the invitation was offered at the end of Friday night campfire message: "If you believe in Jesus as your Savior, who died on the cross and then rose from the grave three days later, as the Forgiver of your sins, we invite you to come forward during this "invitation song." I'd heard different, but similar, invitations to publicly accept Jesus and be baptized in Christ many times.

However, this was *my* time. I also knew I could go to Heaven when I died, if Jesus was my Savior. So ... I went forward, verbally confessed, "I believe that Jesus is the Christ, the Son of the Living God," and celebrated with church camp leaders and fellow campers. *Some* were baptized that very night. I wanted to do so, at my church on Sunday.

After a night of joy, we returned home on Saturday morning. A family picked up my sister and me at church and took us to their home. Shortly after getting there, they told my sister and me that our Daddy had "passed away," very early that morning. He was thirty-three years old and we'd lived in Clovis, New Mexico, for two months, where my dad was the preacher of that little church of seventy-five people.

Honestly, I wasn't as upset as my sister. She was fourteen. I was nine. When they told us he "passed away," I DID NOT UNDERSTAND that he had died ... you see, he was in and out of hospitals throughout those nine years I'd been alive. In fact, he was in the hospital on March 3, 1954, when I was born in Georgia Baptist Hospital in Atlanta, Georgia.

He had osteomyelitis, an infection that deteriorated the bones. He had five back surgeries by the time he was thirty years old. In 1960, his condition was still a bit of a mystery. He'd been to Mayo Clinic twice, to determine exactly the nature of his condition and how to treat it. In 2017, an antibiotic does the trick, but not in the 50s and 60s.

In those first nine years, we'd moved from Georgia to West Virginia to Indiana to New Mexico! (Six different small churches in nine years.) As I said, he'd been in and out of hospitals for those nine years: for treatment to deal with his physical pain … and … in drug rehab to overcome his addiction to pain medications. (I did not understand his addiction to pain meds, but I DID know that he was in deep pain and had "passed out" many times.)

I share this to help you understand why it did not register that "passed away" meant he had died. (I just thought those two words "passed away" were another way of saying, "passed out.")

Side note: That is why I encourage adults to say the words: "He has died" or "He has gone to Heaven" … when telling a child the news that a loved one or friend is gone, never to be seen in this life again. (Not to be harsh but to be clear!) We'll go back to 1963, at the end of this chapter.

Nevertheless, that weekend turned out to be a "defining moment" in my life. I *had* accepted Jesus as my Savior on Friday. I eventually grasped the truth: my dad died on Saturday. I was baptized on Sunday! (The day *after* my dad physically died, I experienced a death as well, into the death, burial and resurrection of Jesus.)

RESTORING ME

Romans 6:3-4 reads, "Or have you forgotten that when we were joined with Christ Jesus in baptism, we joined him in his death? For we died and were buried with Christ by baptism. And just as Christ was raised from the dead by the glorious power of the Father, now we also may live new lives" (NLT).

Although I didn't fully grasp the significance of my baptism that Sunday morning, Romans 6:7-11 reads, "For when we died with Christ we were set free from the power of sin. And since we died with Christ, we know we will also live with him. We are sure of this because Christ was raised from the dead, and he will never die again. Death no longer has any power over him. When he died, he died once to break the power of sin. But now that he lives, he lives for the glory of God. So you also should consider yourselves to be dead to the power of sin and alive to God through Christ Jesus" (NLT).

ALIVE TO GOD! We tend to find our identity in a name ... where we grew up ... the color of our skin ... how we spend our time ... what we believe. *Romans 6:11* suggests we find our identity, not in our biological name, but we are *"alive to God through Jesus Christ."*

Ephesians 1:5 reads, "God decided in advance to adopt us into his own family by bringing us to himself through Jesus Christ" (NLT).

Regardless of our family history, color of skin, the biological name we wear, or even how we spend our time, believers in Jesus find our identity in God. We have been ... ADOPTED!

Adopted! The very word stirs up a variety of emotions. I have always admired those families who have "legally adopted" children into their immediate family. However, before the year 2017, I had never REALLY understood the gift an adopted child was to the adoptive family, nor had I understood the gift that child had been given from the God of the universe: The Gift of Identity.

When our son and daughter-in-law recently officially adopted a precious one-year-old girl from India, our new granddaughter wore the Reeves' name ... *Everly Sairah Reeves!*

After a year's worth of planning the many details necessary to complete the process, the OK required to adopt a child from India, her mom, dad, "Gigi" and especially "Papa" (that's me) would tell anyone that she was worth it all!

When she is a few years older, she will have a healthy sense of worth that her very identity is a result of being added to an immediate family. Her identity has been Restored!

Do you realize that when we come to know Jesus, we are adopted into *His* forever family?

By the way, that is a very good thing because we *all* have a need to belong.

We were born in the image of God, *but* when we choose to disobey God, we cut ourselves *off* from the Lord.

When Jesus becomes the Forgiver of our sins and the Leader of our lives, our Identity is Restored.

We were adopted by God the Father

A movie released in the summer of 2017 was based on a true story. It was entitled *Megan Leavey*. Her life was broken; she had just lost a good friend, who died of alcohol and a drug overdose. Her mother had an affair with her dad's best friend. She was aimless, had no purpose or vision for life. So ... she joined the Marines and became the handler for one of the Marines' trained dogs. "Rex" could smell explosives ... saving many lives in Afghanistan.

But one day, Megan and Rex were injured ... and Megan received a Purple Heart ... But Rex had become more than a tool to sniff out explosives ... Rex became her new "best friend." The unconditional love that a dog can give will do that. Eventually, Megan was able to adopt Rex. (She needed him and he needed her.)

Here's the truth: God didn't need us ... we needed Him. ... When Jesus becomes the Forgiver of our sins and the Leader of our lives, we are *Restored* back to God. Adopted!

God planned our adoption before creation

Ephesians 1:4, "Even before he made the world, God loved us and chose us in Christ to be holy and without fault in his eyes" (NLT).

He knew we'd be cut off from Him by our choice to sin, but He planned to send Jesus to be the Sacrifice for our sins.

God knows us better than we know us ... and yet He still chose to adopt us.

He listens intently when we talk. In fact, even though we often don't think about God, He is always thinking about us. I have heard God described as a proud parent. He's crazy about us. If God had a refrigerator, our picture would be on his "fridge."

It matters that He restored our identity because that influences our decisions. To my sons, particularly during their teen years, I would always tell them before they left the house: "Remember who you are." Now that our youngest son is married and has a child, and now that my wife and I are semi-retired, whenever we leave town, he will always say to me, "Dad, remember who you are!" (Like I could possibly embarrass him or the family name.)

When you are adopted, the God who is your Father, wants you to "remember who you are!" You're *His* son or daughter!

And He loved us before our adoptive or biological parents loved us!

Did you hear that? When you let this truth sink into your soul, that is very empowering and encouraging. You may have grown up without ever hearing your father say, "I love you." But your *eternal* Father in Heaven loved you, before the world even existed!

You ask, "I thought God came up with the plan to forgive, *after* Adam and Eve sinned."

He loved you before anything or anyone existed. He predetermined that He would make a way for us to be adopted by Him and be with Him forever in Heaven one day!

God planned our adoption so we could be set free

John 8:36 says, "If the Son sets you free, you are truly free" (NLT).

Sin separated us from God. (So ... we were orphans!) And until a person is adopted by God the Father, we are slaves to sin and slaves to the system of this world ...with no hope. But when we are adopted into God's Family, we are free from the consequences of sin, free to live with purpose and free to have eternal life with Him, after we leave this world.

God planned our adoption for a purpose

God has supernatural plans for our lives. He wants to use us right now. **He adopted us so that we could tell others of God's plan to adopt them.** When people live without purpose, they aren't really living, they're just existing. "What's the use? Who cares? I'm just exhausted with my mundane, meaningless life."

King Solomon said in Ecclesiastes 1:2,8,9,11, "Everything is meaningless .... No matter how much we see, we are never satisfied. No matter how much we hear, we are not content. History merely repeats itself. It has all been done before. Nothing under the sun is truly new. We don't remember what happened in the past, and in future generations, no one will remember what we are doing now" (NLT). This was a guy who had 1,000 women at his disposal, more power than any political leader today, and more money than the richest person on our planet!

Does he sound like he's living?

Don't miss the point: when life just consists of satisfying ourselves, we have no meaning.

You are a son or daughter of The Most High King ... and He wants to place in your heart a desire to tell others of His amazing love! (That's why you exist!)

God planned our adoption as a part of His plan to restore the world

Christ will set up His kingdom one day, and there will be a new Heaven and a new earth. And all the death, destruction, pain, and sin will no longer exist.

It is so easy to dwell on what's wrong about the world and with us.

But God, by adopting us, has invited us to participate with Him in the process of restoration and enjoy His *new* creation. No matter what you are going through right now, or will have to overcome in the future, you can anticipate the eternal life and future that is to come!

So ... We're adopted by the Father ... And ...

WE ARE RESTORED BY GOD THE SON

Notice Ephesians 1:6-7, "So we praise God for the glorious grace he has poured out on us who belong to his dear Son. He is so rich in kindness and grace that he purchased our freedom with the blood of his Son and forgave our sins" (NLT).

The *NIV* translates Ephesians 1:11, "In Him we were also chosen, having been predestined according to the plan of Him ..." (NIV).

What does it mean, when it says, He "predestined" us?

Well, you cannot understand predestination without discussing God's foreknowledge: Romans 8:29, "For those God foreknew he also predestined to be conformed to the image of his Son ..." (NIV). If God has foreknowledge, He knows, in advance, exactly how we will respond. So ... since He can see into the future, He knows right now if you're going to be in Heaven, after this life. The word "predestination" is used five times in the Bible … And it always speaks of those who choose to love and obey God. Romans 10:13 says, "For 'Everyone who calls on the name of the LORD will be saved'" (NLT).

He chose to adopt us but we have to choose to call on Him as our Father, Savior, and Leader.

In Matthew 16:15, Jesus asked His disciples, (and us), "…Who do you say I am?" (NLT)

Your life and your eternal destiny hangs in the balance, depending on how you answer that question. You will never be asked a more important question: Because that answer will determine what we will do in this life and where we will spend eternity.

So … who is Jesus? How will you choose to answer that question? I can tell you this: No other recognized religious leader ever claimed to be God. Not Moses, Buddha, Confucius or Mohammed!

Jesus is the Only One who ever said or proved to the world that He is God.

Jesus said in John 14:9, "…Anyone who has seen me has seen the Father! …" He went on in John 14:11, "Just believe that I am in the Father and the Father is in me. Or at least believe because of the work you have seen me do" (NLT).

His claim can either be true or false. If false, Jesus either knew His claims were false and He lied, or he was deluded and out of His mind. If He knowingly lied, He's the world's greatest hypocrite and the world's greatest fool. (Because He died for a lie, if He wasn't really the Son of God.)

Here's another question: If He was delusional, how could He help so many people for such a long time? Even His critics and enemies respected His character. At Jesus' trial, Pilate said, "I find no fault in this man."

WE ARE EMPOWERED BECAUSE OF GOD THE HOLY SPIRIT

Ephesians 1:13, "And now you Gentiles have also heard the truth, the Good News that God saves you. And when you believed in Christ, he identified you as his own by giving you the Holy Spirit, whom he promised long ago" (NLT).

When the Holy Spirit comes into our lives, we have a new identity. He "identifies us as His own." God knows us, but how do we get to know Him?

By studying the life of Christ in the Gospels, and being guided by the Holy Spirit, we go from knowing about God to knowing God.

My wife was a huge fan of Johnny Bench, the Hall of Fame catcher for the Big Red Machine in the 70s. (She has all kinds of "Johnny Bench stuff.")

We recently "downsized" and I had to throw or give away many files and books. (But ALL the memorabilia of #5 is with us in our new home.) When she was in the fifth grade, she could tell you everything about him, but she didn't know him personally. For that, I am grateful, because I would have had no chance!

When we are truly restored back to God, we are filled with the Holy Spirit: (We don't just know facts about Him, we know Him!)

RESTORING THE CHURCH

The apostle Paul believed the Ephesian Christians knew Jesus personally. But he did pray that the Holy Spirit would empower them to know the Lord better.

Why?

The Holy Spirit deepens our knowledge of Christ by giving us godly common sense and insight. Now ... the whole truth is that we are an ongoing work of restoration in progress. And the better we know and are led by the Holy Spirit ... the closer we will be restored back to God.

He guarantees our hope

Ephesians 1:14, "The Spirit is God's guarantee that he will give us the inheritance he promised and that he has purchased us to be his own people" (NLT).

As you look to the future, where do you place your trust?

I like the story of a tourist who came too close to the edge of the Grand Canyon, lost his footing and slipped over the side. Just before he fell, he grabbed a bush with both hands. He called, "Is there anybody up there?" A calm voice came out of the sky, "Yes, there is!" ... "Can you help me?" ...

"Yes, I can, but you must have faith." … "Oh yes, I have faith!" … "OK! Then let go of the bush and I'll catch you." After a tense pause, the tourist yelled, "Is anybody else up there?"

Ephesians 1:18, "I pray that your hearts will be flooded with light so that you can understand …"

It's hard to see things that are yet to come. But when you see God work, in real time, that is a reminder that the best is yet to come!

He guides us in the truth

Ephesians 1:18 says, (the Holy Spirit gives us) "…the confident hope he has given … his holy people who are his rich and glorious inheritance" (NLT).

An inheritance is no good if you waste it or misspend it. But the Holy Spirit shows us how to spend our spiritual blessings wisely ... because the Holy Spirit gives us love, joy, peace, patience, kindness, goodness, faithfulness, gentleness, and self-control.

There's one more way the Holy Spirit empowers us:

He teaches us that we have the same power as Jesus

Ephesians 1:19-20, "I also pray that you will understand the incredible greatness of God's power for us who believe him. This is the same mighty power that raised Christ from the dead…" (NLT).

Please know that He breathes life into people, and the church, even if it feels like the power is dead.

I served as lead pastor at Connection Pointe Christian Church from June 1986 through September 2017. The church experienced eight years of numerical decline from 1978 to 1986 … from an attendance of over 600 to 200. (Church splits, staff members who surrendered to public sin, one pastor was voted out of the church, and one was let go because, for a year and a half, the church declined from 400 to 200 people.)

There was only one new member, a membership transfer from another church, in over a nine-month period from September '85 to June '86.

The church had been so wounded, she was like an abused child … like an orphan ... who needed to be Adopted!

The Holy Spirit establishes Christ as the Head of the Church, and He alone can pour love into God's people.

Then … Relationships are restored! Obstacles are overcome! Broken bodies are healed! Grieving hearts are comforted! Anxious minds are calmed. And people without hope are adopted, restored and empowered by God the Father, the Son and the Holy Spirit!!!

And that is the heart of Paul's prayer for the Ephesian church, every congregation and follower of Christ.

Let's revisit the history of the Church worldwide.

In 30 A.D. – The Church exploded on the day of Pentecost in Jerusalem and people from seventeen linguistic groups heard the Good News in their own language. They surrendered to Christ and 3,000 were baptized on the spot.

In 38 A.D. – The apostle Peter travels to Caesarea to the home of an Italian soldier named Cornelius. He was the first non-Jewish person to be led to Christ. And when that racial barrier shattered, it launched a global expansion of the Kingdom of God.

In 42 A.D. – The apostle Mark went south to Egypt.

In 49 A.D. – The apostle Paul goes north to Turkey.

In 51 A.D. – Paul left Turkey to go west to Greece. And the apostle John moves to Turkey with Mary, the mother of Jesus. She'd die in John's home in Ephesus.

In 52 A.D. – The apostle Thomas heads to India where the Gospel literally transformed the sociology of the southern half of India.

In 54 A.D. – The apostle Paul launches his third and final missionary journey where he dies a martyr's death in prison. (But before he's beheaded, he leads a number of prison guards to Jesus.)

In 432 A.D. – Patrick heads to Ireland to take the Gospel to people on the Emerald Isle. And we celebrate that missionary, every year, by dressing in green and getting smashed! (I'm not sure Patrick would approve, but that's how we roll in this culture!)

By the 1800's – Seven out of ten Americans claimed to be Methodists, as John Wesley led a revival throughout the land.

In 1801 – A Presbyterian Pastor named Thomas Campbell, came to the conviction that God called him to be a Christian only. So, he had fellowship with any congregation who acknowledged that Jesus is Lord and the

Authority is the Bible.

And that conviction led to a wave of non-denominational churches that called themselves Christian churches.

They believed the Bible was the guidance of God for every issue, and every congregation had the responsibility to keep their church accountable, to the Bible and the Lordship of Christ. This movement became the fastest growing Christian movement in America in the 1800's. (And that movement spread to central Indiana.)

In 1837, twenty-two followers of Christ met in a log cabin in Brownsburg, Indiana. They began the Brownsburg Christian Church (now in her 180th year, known as Connection Pointe Christian Church). I share that history to clarify that *we* are a church that is part of this Restoration Movement: We are Christians only ... but not the only Christians!

Since He has adopted us, we still wear His name!

During the French Revolution, some men were determined to abolish Christianity. One night, an atheist was loudly declaring his anti-God doctrine, "Everything will be abolished – churches, Bibles, clergymen, even the Word of God itself. We shall remove everything which speaks of religion."

A peasant chuckled, as he pointed to the stars, "I was just wondering how you and your crew would manage to get them down!"

Before God even made the stars, He loved us and chose to adopt us. But God didn't choose to adopt us as His children because of who we are, but because of who He is!

My daughter-in-law, Brooke, sounds a lot like the heart of God, in this message she posted just after getting our new granddaughter from India: "If you haven't yet met Everly Sairah Reeves, she is precious and perfect. A thumb sucker like her mommy was and taking this new world all in. Adoption isn't all rainbows and it isn't all easy. But giving her a forever family is worth the tears (from all of us), every dollar spent, every errand run and every copy made. Everly is a blessed little girl with three families. Her bio family, her orphanage family and now the Reeves/Gilbert family. I can't believe we could have missed this if not for a giant leap of faith, and the prayers and support from so many of you. Thanks for going on this journey with us. It's only the start. There will be good days and bad, but Everly has a forever home and a community of people who will love her like their own."

As it turns out, not only is our personal identity found in Christ, but the same can be said of the church: our Restored Identity assigns us our name: Christian!

Let's briefly pick up my story in 1963.

Naturally, as a 9-year-old whose father had just died, I was *not* thinking about the cause of his death. I just knew that my *heavenly* Father had taken away my *biological* father.

Long story short: my mother, my 14-year-old sister, my 4-year-old brother, and I moved to Cincinnati, Ohio. My mom had gone to college at Cincinnati Christian University and graduated as the valedictorian of the 1946 class. She found a job as an assistant editor at The Standard Publishing Company (a Christian publishing house).

We did not even own a car for the first two years in Cincy. We were poor … but I did not know that. Why?

She found an apartment that was close enough to walk to school. We had good meals … AND … a new church family. She had arranged for three different families to pick us up for Sunday morning, Sunday evening, and Wednesday night church.

I now understand that what Satan meant for evil, grief, and pain, God used for good. The day we arrived, by train, after my father's death, I can remember walking into that apartment as if it were yesterday.

We walked in, looked around, and made our way into the kitchen. As I opened the refrigerator and the cupboards, I saw food, food, and more food!!! I asked, "Where did all this come from?"

I can still hear the answer, fifty-four years later: "This is all from your new church family!" (That church today is The Lifespring Christian Church!) I could not put this together in my mind at that time, but I do know that Psalm 68:5 is true. "His name is the LORD—rejoice in his presence! Father to the fatherless, defender of widows …" (NLT).

My dad had died but I had been *adopted* by my heavenly Father! The process of Restoration had begun in me. My identity was now secure in Christ. As I retire from forty years of full-time pastoral ministry, I am writing my very first book on my *eternal* family, the Church.

Adopted! *Restored …* by God, "Father to the fatherless."

ACTION STEPS FOR OUR STORY

1. Write out when you first realized you needed to be adopted by God.

2. How has God started the work of Restoration in you and your church?

3. What's your next step in your life? In your church?

JESUS' FIRST PRIORITY:
THE CHURCH

A study of Jesus' life and ministry reveals Seven Priorities that inform and guide our understanding of the Church, the first priority being the Church itself. The Church was God's plan for spreading the Gospel to all nations and all of the time and effort that he invested in his disciples were intended to equip and empower them to lead his *Ekklesia*, the "called out" to transform their neighborhood.

Human beings often fail to effectively and consistently execute Christ's vision and that has unfortunately been true of the way they have led the Church since the death of the apostles. "Church" has often been relegated to a building, a program, an association, or an organization - and allowing these misconceptions to take root has had damaging consequences including but not limited to pride, brokenness, division, corruption, and ineffectiveness.

But these failures should not diminish the importance or value of the Church in our mind. Instead, our knowledge of God's Word and our understanding of history should combine to compel us to embrace God's vision for his Church and execute our leadership in accordance with that vision.

CHAPTER TWO

RESTORED UNITY

Honestly, at the time of my dad's death, my most vivid memories of church were *not* of unity and love, but disunity and cruelty. In fairness to these churches, it surely was difficult to be patient and forgiving of a preacher battling addiction to pain medications, and many hospitalizations.

However, a few months before his death, I remember sitting in the front row of a congregational meeting when my dad was publicly ridiculed and literally thrown out of the church. My naïve understanding of the church was deeply scarred. "Church people" were mean, insensitive, dare I say, "non-Christian,"at least to the eyes and ears of a nine-year-old preacher's kid.

Shortly thereafter, we moved from the Midwest to New Mexico, where as described in chapter one, he died in two months. Clearly, I had lost Christ's description of the Church, in my heart. It needed to be restored!

Ephesians 2:13-14, "But now you have been united with Christ Jesus. Once you were far away from God, but now you have been brought near to him through the blood of Christ. For Christ himself has brought peace to us. He united Jews and Gentiles into one people when, in his own body on the cross, he broke down the wall of hostility that separated us" (NLT).

What's the first word that comes to mind when you hear, "church people"? My guess is this: Your church experiences most often define how you think of church people. Survey after survey suggest that those outside the church describe us as "judgmental, prejudiced, prideful, arrogant, mean-spirited, isolated, contentious, divided" (to name only a few).

Unfortunately, those words are not only used to describe "church people" by the unchurched, but by those now dechurched or even regular church attenders. To many individuals the words, "church unity" are an oxymoron. (They do *not* go together.)

That *should* serve as a "wake-up call" to those who claim to love Jesus and His Church. After all, Jesus' *real* prayer is recorded in John 17:9-11, "My prayer is not for the world, but for those you have given me, because they belong to you. All who are mine belong to you, and you have given them to me, so they bring me glory. Now I am departing from the world; they are staying in this world, but I am coming to you. Holy Father, you have given me your name; now protect them by the power of your name so that they will be united just as we are" (NLT).

RESTORING ME

To be restored is "to have someone or something that has been taken or lost, returned to you." To be "brought back, reestablished, *restored*."

That is our story! It is my story! It is the story of the Church! *RESTORED UNITY*.

Throughout my ministry I have used jokes to set up or reaffirm a main point. My kids call them "dad jokes." Hope you enjoy!

Two moose hunters who flew to Anchorage, Alaska, and then they got on a small single engine plane and flew deep into the tundra. The pilot found a dirt runway, and as they were circling to land, he said to these two moose hunters, "Now, I can only take back one moose. If I take back two, I won't have room for your gear." He let them off and came back a week later. He circled the runway and, sure enough, there they were … each had a moose. He was so disgusted, and after landing, he said, "I told you we could only take one moose." They said, "We came out here last year and we both got a moose. We came in the same size plane and that pilot let us bring 'em both."

The pilot said, "Well, I'm as good a pilot as that man … if he can do it, I can do it."

He shoved in all the gear, squeezed in both animals and the hunters … shut the door. He got down to the end of the runway and took off. They lifted off, but didn't quite make it … they hit a tree. The plane went flying and after the dust settled … one of the hunters stuck his head up through the limbs of the tree and said, "Where are we?" The other stuck his head up and said, "I'm not sure, but I think we're about 150 yards further than last year."

Unfortunately we don't always learn from the past. I also like the cartoon that pictures a pastor, sitting in his office. He has a look of panic on his face, while obviously seeking counsel on the phone. Five members of the church board barge into his office, and the caption reads: "Bad news, Pastor, our church planting team is *divided* on whether to call the new congregation 'First United Church' or 'United First Church.'"

We just don't learn from history, do we? You've heard this: "If you don't learn from history, you're bound to repeat it."

RESTORING THE CHURCH

Connection Pointe Christian Church is a work of Restoration *in progress*. We aren't there yet, and won't be *fully* restored until we are with the Lord in Heaven. Ephesians 4:3 gives us a picture of what Restoration looks like. "Make every effort to keep yourselves united in the Spirit, binding yourselves together with peace" (NLT).

The movement to Restore God's vision
for the Church is a unity movement

Throughout the Middle Ages, the church drifted from the truth. A number of reformers emerged: Martin Luther, John Calvin, John Knox, John Wesley. They emphasized a *return* to biblical truth.

The result, however, was *division*. Each had their own creed ... their own denominational structure. By 1800, the division was so great that the truth was difficult to discern.

Another movement began about that time, in America, with the purpose of restoring basic, simple New Testament Christianity. Thomas and Alexander Campbell, Barton W. Stone, Walter Scott began to speak of unity.

Their vision was to restore the truth but also be united, so they declared. "No creed but Christ. No book of authority but the Bible." To avoid being divided by names, they said, "We shall be called Christians only." Acts 11:26 reads, "(It was at Antioch that the believers were first called Christians)" (NLT). For a time, this "Restoration" movement was the fastest growing movement in America.

Unfortunately, a three-fold division occurred around 1900. (Nearly every religious movement can be divided three ways: the conservative, the moderate, the more liberal.)

A movement that began seeking unity became divided.

Divided over missions

Up to this point, every church in the Bible was independent. The church at Antioch had no authority over the church at Ephesus. All of the churches were independent, which meant the missions support was independent too.

That has some advantages. It eliminates "red tape." You don't have to pay for any missions organization, personnel or building. Every dollar given goes directly to the church who then gives directly to missions, outside the church's walls.

The other advantage is that there is direct involvement. You can know what is going on in that mission. (If you send the money to a mission *organization*, you may have no idea where the money is going.)

But there are also some disadvantages:

The missionary is totally responsible for his support. When he comes back for a furlough, he has to go to all these places to reaffirm his support. By the time the furlough is over, he is exhausted.

And there is often a *lack* of accountability.

Since there was this problem of accountability, they established an organization called the United Christian Missionary Society. Rather than sending their money overseas, they decided to send it to the U.C.M.S. (They would screen the missionary, and keep them accountable.)

Some saw that as an advantage. Others, however, saw that as a danger because, it could eventually become a denomination.

Churches became divided over whether to send money to the U.C.M.S. or to the mission field *directly*.

Now, generally speaking, those who cooperated with the U.C.M.S. considered themselves Christian Churches ("Disciples of Christ").

In time, the "Disciples of Christ" came to believe that immersion for baptism was no longer required for membership or to serve on the mission field.

Eventually, they began to question the authority of the Scriptures, the virgin birth, the resurrection of Jesus. (Connection Pointe became *independent* in 1957, because of these liberal views of Scripture.)

In the early 1960s, this group called the Disciples of Christ, no longer claiming to be an independent movement, set up a headquarters in Indianapolis with delegates to a convention and a President of the church. They set up a structure that would enable them to merge later, with other denominations.

At about the same time, another division surfaced. This one had been brewing ever since the Civil War. They had …

Divided over musical instruments

Some argued that the organ or the piano wasn't authorized in the New Testament. While the Old Testament talked about a variety of instruments used to praise God and while the New Testament talked about instruments in Heaven, the New Testament, they said, did not say anything about the use of a piano or an organ in worship.

(It should not be used.)

Others insisted that since the New Testament did not mention these instruments, we should have freedom. (The instrument can enhance worship.)

(Liberalism undermines the church but legalism stifles.)

Recently a large church was arguing over whether to wear choir robes. The Pastor came and prayed, "Lord, help us to be wise enough to not drown in *shallow* water."

There's an old story about a church just after the Civil War that was divided over the use of the piano in worship. (Half wanted it and half didn't.)

The half that wanted it, bought one, and when they came in one Sunday, there it was on the platform. The other half was furious. They came back the next Sunday and the piano was gone. They couldn't find it … searched for months. Six months later they found it … You know where? In the baptistery!

The moral is this: when you are divided over things like that in the church, you *aren't* going to be using the baptistery very much. Brownsburg Christian Church started in 1837, but a group split from the church in 1890, over musical instruments.

(What does the Bible say?)

Psalm 150 says, "Praise the LORD! Praise God in his sanctuary; praise him in his mighty Heaven! Praise him for his mighty works; praise his unequaled greatness! Praise him with a blast of the ram's horn; praise him with the lyre and harp! Praise him with the tambourine and dancing; praise him with strings and flutes! Praise him with a clash of cymbals; praise him with loud clanging cymbals. Let everything that breathes sing praises to the LORD! Praise the Lord!" (NLT)

God was pleased with the use of instruments in the Old Testament. Revelation 5:8 talks about the elders around the throne of God: "…Each one had a harp…"

Why this history lesson?

Ephesians 4:3 answers that question: "Make every effort to keep the unity of the Spirit through the bond of peace" (NIV).

Connection Pointe is a non-denominational Christian Church

Our goal is to speak the truth (restore New Testament Christianity) in love.

Ephesians 4:15-16, "Instead, we will speak the truth in love, growing in every way more and more like Christ, who is the head of his body, the church. He makes the whole body fit together perfectly. As each part does its own special work, it helps the other parts grow, so that the whole body is healthy and growing and full of love" (NLT).

Unity is a reflection of what we believe

Ephesians 2:1-3, "Once you were dead because of your disobedience and your many sins. You used to live in sin, just like the rest of the world, obeying the devil—the commander of the powers in the unseen world. He is the spirit at work in the hearts of those who refuse to obey God. All of us used to live that way, following the passionate desires and inclinations of our sinful nature. By our very nature we were subject to God's anger, just like everyone else" (NLT).

The writer makes an assumption: "You *used* to be like the rest of the world." If you've become a Christian, your life *should* be different than it used to be. (But you still can be dead spiritually and not realize it.)

Did you know that when you are freezing to death, you actually *feel* warm and can die in a storm, because you go to sleep and it feels so good?

That is why feeling "comfortable" does not mean you're restored spiritually. (What you believe is *not* based on feelings.)

Ephesians 2:4-5, "God is so rich in mercy, and he loved us so much, that even though we were dead because of our sins, he gave us life when he raised Christ from the dead. (It is only by God's grace that you have been saved!)" (NLT)

This is the core belief of Christianity. And that is good news for us! Ephesians 2:6, "For he raised us from the dead along with Christ and seated us with him in the Heavenly realms because we are united with Christ Jesus" (NLT).

Loving the One True God and loving others as one is the DNA of the Church.

Years ago, a Christian slave in America was groaning, weeping, and praying to the Lord for deliverance from Satan. The slave owner said, "Why are you asking to be delivered from the devil? The devil never bothers me. You're a praying Christian, I am not … Why does the devil bother you?"

The African American man said, "When you're shooting ducks, which do you send your dog after first? The dead ones or the wounded ones, trying to get away?"

"I send the dog to the wounded ones. We can pick up the dead ones later" The slave said, "Satan already has those who are not followers of Christ. But the ones who know the Lord are the ones Satan sends his dogs after. He can pick up the already dead ones later."

Years ago, at a conference comparing Christianity with other religions, someone mentioned that God took on human form in Jesus … But other religions also believe God appears in other human forms. But then the resurrection came up: Death is not final. The tomb of Jesus was and is empty. But someone said, "Other religions have accounts of people returning from the dead."

But then, C.S. Lewis supposedly walked in and asked what the debate was about. When he was told that they were debating what's unique about Christianity, he suggested that Christians believe God's love is free, while other religions are based on what you do *for* God.

Whether he said that or not, it is true … *Buddhists* follow an eight-fold path to enlightenment. *Hindus* believe in karma (your actions determine how the world treats you.) The *Jewish code* of the law implies that God has *requirements* for people to be accepted by God. *Islam* sees God as a God of judgement, rather than as a God of love.

Only *Christianity* proclaims that God's love is *unconditional*. Grace is all about God freely giving us forgiveness, mercy and love. So, unity reflects what we believe …

Unity is a recognition of differences

You may ask, "What does this have to do with unity?" Look again at Ephesians 2:14, "For Christ himself has brought peace to us. He united Jews and Gentiles into one people when, in his own body on the cross, he broke down the wall of hostility that separated us" (NLT).

When we are Restored, in Christ, "the walls of hostility are broken down." Christianity Restores unity, in that we not only *recognize* differences, but we are determined to *reach out* to people of all religions and races.

As God continues to Restore a church, they will become more and more *diverse*. (Across generations and across racial divides.)

A few years ago, our mostly Caucasian congregation started serving alongside a mostly African American congregation. We were united in our core beliefs: The Bible as our authority, Jesus as God in flesh, virgin born, died as the Substitute for our sins, and rose from the dead, three days after His crucifixion.

However, we were not united. We were located in "the burbs," they were located in "the hood." Frankly, the racial division (between Jews and Gentiles) referred to in Ephesians 2 was even more intense than the tension between "whites" and "blacks" in America in 2017. However, we must be as *intentional* to reach across racial lines, in our day, as the apostle Paul was in declaring that the Good News of Jesus was for Jews and Gentiles.

One of the greatest blessings of my forty years in pastoral ministry has occurred these last few years: The pastor of the "New Era Church" and the pastor of "Connection Pointe Christian Church" have become like "brothers from another mother."

(That's how my friend, Pastor Clarence Moore, refers to me.) He has become one of my closest friends. We speak at each other's congregations, have traveled thousands of miles to attend pastors' conferences with each other, meet most weeks with no agenda, other than to be together. We have never greeted each other without a warm physical embrace. We have shared personal struggles, sermon ideas, leadership lessons and ministry challenges at our congregations.

There are no areas of our lives that are "off limits." There is a safety between us that frees us up to share the last 10% with each other. We trust each other, understand each other, and love each other!

Bluntly stated: If pastors are not willing to intentionally cultivate authentic relationships with pastors from other races, a church may claim to follow the Bible, but they are *not* Restoring the Church of the New Testament!

I have heard, over the last forty years, that the most difficult challenge for the Church is to become racially diverse. I get it ... I've heard and studied the challenges of crossing racial lines, but we can no longer fail to make this a MAJOR priority of leading a church to "Restored Unity."

In fact, Pastor Clarence Moore and I, God willing, want to spend our "post local pastor" seasons of ministry, traveling the country, challenging churches and leaders to be led by the Holy Spirit of God and intentionally act on what God has declared in His Word.

Again, Ephesians 2:14, "...Christ himself has brought peace to us. He united Jews and Gentiles (people with different skin colors) into one people ... He broke down the wall of hostility that separated us" (NLT).

He has already done the work, we must not only believe it, but *live* like it.

When God Restores us, through the grace and mercy of Christ, we will be very intentional to give grace and mercy to others, especially those of other races. Just remember: a person does not have to be my twin to be my brother or sister.

William Whiting Borden was a Christian missionary to Egypt, from November 1, 1887 to April 9, 1913. William Borden was the heir to the Borden, Inc. family fortune. He was a graduate of Yale University in 1909 and Princeton Theological Seminary.

Borden was converted under the ministry of Dwight Moody. He later became a missionary to the Muslims in China, but died in Egypt of spinal meningitis at age twenty-five. After his death, they found his Bible and gave it to his parents.

They found in one place "No Reserve," and a date shortly after he renounced his fortune to go into missions. Later, in his Bible he wrote, "No Retreat," dated shortly after his father told him he would never let him work in the company again. Just before he died in Egypt, he added, "No Regrets."

Now, why did William Borden decide "No Reserve, No Retreat, No Regrets," and go to do mission work for Jesus in China?

Because of what he believed about Jesus, because he embraced the truth that Christ brought peace and broke down the walls of hostility that separate us ... and because he'd matured in his faith enough to know that we are all His, carefully joined together in Him!

Ephesians 2:16-18, "Together as one body, Christ reconciled both groups to God by means of his death on the cross, and our hostility toward each other was put to death. He brought this Good News of peace to you Gentiles who were far away from him, and peace to the Jews who were near. Now all of us can come to the Father through the same Holy Spirit because of what Christ has done for us" (NLT).

The only way to God is through Jesus Christ. Regardless of anyone's *cultural/religious* background, they can find grace, peace and eternal life through Jesus.

Restored unity is a reflection of what we believe, and restored unity embraces diversity in the body of Christ, the Church.

Unity is the result of maturity

Ephesians 2:19-21, "So now you Gentiles are no longer strangers and foreigners. You are citizens along with all of God's holy people. You are members of God's family. Together, we are his house, built on the foundation of the apostles and the prophets. And the cornerstone is Christ Jesus himself. We are carefully joined together in him, becoming a holy temple for the Lord" (NLT).

Notice, through our core belief in Jesus, people with all kinds of differences are welcome to be a part of His family ... the Church!

ACTION STEPS FOR OUR STORY

We must see every person in light of their spiritual potential.

We must see ourselves in light of God's desire to embrace the world through us.

Why? Because we are "a holy temple for the Lord ..."

When His love takes root in us and in the church, God's miraculous work of Restoration makes us alive in Christ!

Ephesians 2:6, "For he raised us from the dead along with Christ and seated us with him in the Heavenly realms because we are united with Christ Jesus" (NLT).

Through His great love for us, He has "seated us in the Heavenly realms in Christ Jesus."

Don't miss this: A united church is mature and that enables the church to be healthy and stable.

1. What is your next step to becoming united with those who are different than you?
2. What is keeping you from intentionally crossing racial lines?
3. How can your church move toward unity, health and maturity?

We took two major steps to be more inclusive and united as a church.

The very FIRST week on the new campus, we had cars parked everywhere. We had not paved the front part of our parking lot. So ... on Monday, the elders met and made a $100,000 decision! Just like that! We had it paved, immediately! When the people arrived the SECOND week, there was ample parking. We told the congregation, "We did not pave the front lot before last week. We planned to do it, as soon as we needed it." (Remember, we moved from a 2-acre site to a 118-acre site.) We didn't have it paved, because we couldn't afford it.

God showed us that we couldn't afford to *NOT* pave the front lot, IF we REALLY wanted to reach others, beyond our little community of Brownsburg. So ... we paved the lot on Monday, the very next day after our opening weekend!

When the congregation arrived on Sunday, we said, "Do you like our newly paved front lot? The elders decided on Monday to pave it because God sent many new people to us last week, from many other communities. This was a test: Do we REALLY want to connect ALL people to Jesus, even if they are different than us? After prayer, we arranged to have it paved BEFORE this Sunday. Now, we need to pay for it. We need $100,000, over and above our regular giving, next Sunday! Any questions?"

Can you believe that the congregation gave MORE than $100,000, over and above regular giving, that very next Sunday?

Here's the second MAJOR step we took to be more inclusive and united as a church: We changed the name of the church, that had been known as Brownsburg Christian Church for 164 years! Three years after our relocation, we had more people attending who lived *outside* of Brownsburg than in Brownsburg. At one time, Brownsburg had a bit of a reputation as being racist.

So ... We changed our name to reflect the fact that we were now a regional church, not just a community church. And ... because of the racial connotation the name of Brownsburg had among some people in our region. We saw ourselves as simply a "Connection Pointe" – connecting people of all ages, communities, and races to this Restored, united church family!

We were experiencing Restored Unity ... And those two decisions had a lot to do with our growing from a church of 1,500 to over 4,000 in the next fifteen years!

JESUS' SECOND PRIORITY: TRANSFORMING THE NEIGHBORHOOD

The second of the Seven Priorities of Jesus is his focus on Transforming the Neighborhood.

Jesus invested a significant amount of his time out and about on hillsides, in communities, and in homes. He could have stayed exclusively in the Temple courts. He could have established a new physical location that would serve as the place to come and experience the always impressive interactions between Jesus and the teachers of the law, between Jesus and the demons, between Jesus and the skeptics, and between Jesus and the disciples.

He did neither of these things, though and instead modeled an outward focus – a relentless commitment to moving among the people in the neighborhood to demonstrate the power of the Gospel and the perfect love that is available through His ministry and eventual death, burial, and resurrection.

But the priority Jesus placed on the neighborhood was more than just a preference of proximity and ministry context. It was an intentional strategy to demonstrate there is no room for isolationism or an "us versus them" mentality. He broke down perceived barriers. He sought to generate fundamental changes in the lives of people outside of any building and more importantly outside a saving relationship with God - regardless of their race, culture or status.

He focused on the neighborhood in order to bring them into the realm of the *Ekklesia*.

CHAPTER THREE

RESTORED PLAN

When I spoke to the Connection Pointe Family on my "farewell weekend," September 23-24, 2017, I said, "If you don't think God can use you, because you've messed up too much or been wounded too deeply, I am Exhibit A: God's mysterious plan includes you, no matter how you've failed or how deeply you've been hurt!"

After moving to Cincinnati in 1963, it was tough sledding. I actually received straight D's in conduct, in the fourth and sixth grades, and graciously received C's in conduct in the fifth grade because my teacher told my mom she sympathized with my lack of a dad.

I have *no* doubt that my teachers did *not* think I had much leadership potential. But God really *can* do more than we can ever ask or imagine!

That is perhaps why the apostle Paul used the word "mysterious" to describe God's miraculous plan of restoration for "emotionally challenged" fourth grade boys and even the most dysfunctional of churches. God's plan is a mystery and so is much of the Bible.

Have you heard of the top ten "mysterious questions" of the Bible? This list looks at some of the historical mysteries and even some of the theological mysteries contained in the Bible, according to ListVerse.com. They are:

10. Where is The Holy Grail?

9. Where is The Ark of the Covenant?

8. Were Sodom and Gomorrah real cities?

7. Where is The Garden of Eden?

6. Are there coded messages in the Bible?

5. What happened to The Lost Tribe?

4. Who was The Pharaoh of The Exodus?

3. Where is Noah's Ark?

2. Who was The Beloved Disciple?

1. Who wrote The Gospels?

While those are interesting and mysterious questions, our focus in this chapter will be on His mysterious plan for each of us and every church.

Do these questions peak your curiosity? Puzzles, secret plots, and mysteries are almost an obsession, if movie and television titles are any indication.

If you'd like to read about these top ten mysteries of the Bible, Google is ready to deliver.

RESTORING ME

The greatest mystery of all history is unveiled in Ephesians 3: *God's Mysterious Plan* for you and me!

We would never know God's mysterious plan *unless* God revealed it to us. The story of Jesus <u>was</u> a secret until God pulled back the curtain.

However, we will never *experience* God's work of Restoration unless we surrender to Him!

Ephesians 3:3 reads, "As I briefly wrote earlier, God himself revealed his mysterious plan to me" (NLT).

HIS MYSTERIOUS PLAN IS BORN OUT OF PRAYER

Ephesians 3:4, "As you read what I have written, you will understand my insight into this plan regarding Christ" (NLT).

When the Church began in Acts 2, the Holy Spirit came to men and women in the Greco-Roman world, but they were all Jews. But in Caesarea, Gentiles received the same Spirit. Ephesians 3:6, "And this is God's plan: Both Gentiles and Jews who believe the Good News share equally in the riches inherited by God's children" (NLT).

All people are welcome

Gentiles, as well as Jews, in Christ, are assured of equal participation in all the blessings and benefits of God's grace.

Dad joke alert. Three people were arguing about what profession was used first in the Bible. The surgeon said, "The medical profession was used first when God took a rib from Adam and created Eve." The engineer said, "No, engineering was used first! Just think of all the engineering it took to create the world out of chaos."

But the politician said, "Listen: You would have nothing, if we didn't create chaos in the beginning."

Politicians often see themselves as men and women of power, but most Americans see them as creating chaos. (Real power comes from God and His plan!)

In West Texas, there was a famous oil field known as Yates Pool. During the Depression, this field was a sheep ranch owned by a man named Yates. Mr. Yates was not able to make enough money on his ranching operation to pay the principle and interest on the mortgage, so he was in danger of losing his ranch. With little money for clothes and food, his family had to live on a government subsidy.

Day after day, as he grazed his sheep, he wondered how he would be able to pay his bills. Then a seismograph crew from an oil company came into the area, and told Mr. Yates that there might be oil on his land. They asked permission to drill a well, and he signed a lease contract.

At 1,115 feet, they struck a huge oil reserve. (80,000 barrels a day) Many of the wells later were twice as large. Thirty years after the first well was drilled, all the wells still had the potential of pumping 125,000 barrels of oil a day! The day Mr. Yates purchased the property, he received all the oil and mineral rights ... but he was living on government assistance. A multi-millionaire, living in poverty! (He owned it, but he did not know it.)

Regardless of your spiritual or racial heritage, all God's blessings are available, but we don't even realize it! So ... How do we find out about all that He offers to us? (Through prayer!)

Look at Ephesians 3:6, "Both are part of the same body, and both enjoy the promise of blessings because they belong to Christ Jesus" (NLT).

When we pray, we realize that …

All members are part of the same body

The word for "body" that Paul uses is used *only here* in the New Testament. (It's not found in classical Greek.) He melded two Greek words: *Su,* meaning *"together with."* *Soma,* the word for *"body."*

In science, *soma* is the word used to describe all the cells and tissues in the body collectively, except germ cells. We are not all the same in function or form, but we all are *essential* parts of the body.

Do you see the mystery? To God, we are fellow members in the body of Christ, the Church. The mind of Christ is the one brain which should control us all. Paul continues in Ephesians 3:9, "I was chosen to explain to everyone this mysterious plan that God, the Creator of all things, had kept secret from the beginning" (NLT).

Ephesians 3:11 reads, "This was his eternal plan, which he carried out through Christ Jesus our Lord" (NLT).

When we pray to God, we are the same body.

All believers come to God through Christ Jesus *(when we pray)*

The point of Ephesians 3:11 is this: We who are non-Jews are assured we have been a part of God's plan from the beginning. It was not just the "chosen race" of the Hebrews who were privileged to participate in this connection with God, but all people and all races everywhere!

In Ephesians 3:14-16, we see how God revealed His eternal plan to Paul: "When I think of all this, I fall to my knees and pray to the Father, the Creator of everything in heaven and on earth. I pray that from his glorious, unlimited resources he will empower you with inner strength through his Spirit" (NLT).

Prayer has always been the source of insight and power for His people!

How did John Wesley accomplish so much for the Lord? It was the power of prayer!

He traveled 250,000 miles in his lifetime. Preached 40,000 sermons. 400 books. He knew ten languages. At eighty-three, he was annoyed that he could not write more than fifteen hours a day without hurting his eyes. At eighty-six, he was ashamed he couldn't preach more than twice a day. He complained in his diary that there was an increasing tendency to lie in bed until ... 5:30 in the morning!

Reportedly, Abraham Lincoln talked about his need to pray because he had no place else to go.

I wonder why Abraham Lincoln and we do not go to God *first*? Why don't we turn to God *first*, instead of turning to Him as a *last resort*?

Cornelia "Corrie" ten Boom was a Dutch watchmaker and Christian who, along with her family, helped many Jews escape the Nazi Holocaust during World War II. By all accounts, they saved nearly 800 lives. She was imprisoned for her actions.

I like Corrie Ten Boom's question, when she asked if prayer is more like a spare tire or a steering wheel?

In Luke 11:1, we read, "Once Jesus was in a certain place praying. As he finished, one of his disciples came to him and said, "Lord, teach us to pray..." (NLT).

Why did the disciples ask Jesus to teach them to pray? I think they saw that Jesus received *power* through prayer.

There is power through talking with the Father because when we go to Him in prayer, we get to know God's heart and God's mysterious, supernatural plan.

HIS MYSTERIOUS PLAN IS EMPOWERED BY THE HOLY SPIRIT

"...He will empower you with inner strength through his Spirit" (Ephesians 3:16, NLT).

Let's move from the personal to the congregational plan of God.

RESTORING THE CHURCH

The Church is often looking for better methods. God is looking for better leaders. The Holy Spirit does not flow through methods, but through leaders. He does not anoint plans, but leaders!

Jesus said in John 16:7-13, "It is best for you that I go away, because if I don't, the Advocate (Holy Spirit) won't come. If I do go away, then I will send him to you. And when he comes, he will convict the world of its sin, and of God's righteousness, and of the coming judgment. The world's sin is that it refuses to believe in me. Righteousness is available because I go to the Father, and you will see me no more. Judgment will come because the ruler of this world has already been judged." (Satan) "There is so much more I want to tell you, but you can't bear it now. When the Spirit of truth comes, he will guide you into all truth. He will not speak on his own but will tell you what he has heard. He will tell you about the future" (NLT).

Just before Jesus ascended to Heaven, He said in Acts 1:8, "You will receive power when the Holy Spirit comes upon you" (NLT).

Please understand: the *Holy Spirit* can strengthen our inner being or our human *spirit* if we ask for His strength. But what if we don't ask? Does that mean we'll go it alone or without His help?

I don't know! ... But I sure don't want to find out how impossible it would be to share His mysterious plan, with the world, *without* His help!

For people and for churches, the restoration process *will not happen* unless there are tangible victories to *celebrate*, as God's Holy Spirit empowers the supernatural "turnaround."

I have experienced God's restoration in my life and I have seen Him restore the Brownsburg Christian Church, through the power of the Holy Spirit. Following eight straight years of numerical decline, the congregation started to grow again. (The worship attendance grew sixty-five percent from 1986-1987!)

REVIVAL, RENEWAL, RESTORATION

Here's what we did

During a two-month period, we contacted a list of people who'd had some recent contact with the church. A total of 237 visits were made!

We also had a banquet honoring *all* volunteer teachers and leaders, and provided a teacher-training weekend. (Restored churches *encourage* and *equip* their leaders ...)

We also had a "Friend Day" ... that core group of 250 people brought 100 guests on "Friend Day!" We provided a Friendship luncheon for everyone!

Here's How It Helped

After the prolonged period of decline, the morale of the congregation was quite low. However, as a result of this two-month emphasis, the church family was reminded that God's mysterious plan is for everyone, including declining churches!

In those days, we had adult Sunday School classes so we started new classes, targeted to reach specific groups: a young adult class and a class for women who attended without their husbands. You'll read one of those stories later in this chapter.

As the church experienced growth, we publicly celebrated that and hope for the future was restored in the hearts of the church family.

A VISION RESTORED

The growth did not cease *after* the two-month emphasis, as members continued to invite guests to their small groups (Sunday School classes).

In fact, six months *after* the two-month emphasis in March and April, the Sunday School averaged 10% *more* than during March and April!

The late Lyle Schaller said in his book, *Activating the Passive Church*, that it was essential to *celebrate every victory*. If you haven't publicly celebrated recently, please do it soon!

When broken people and churches begin the process of being restored through prayer and the power of the Holy Spirit ... the wounded *experience God's supernatural love!*

HIS MYSTERIOUS PLAN IS ROOTED IN LOVE

Ephesians 3:17-19, "Then Christ will make his home in your hearts as you trust in him. Your roots will grow down into God's love and keep you strong. And may you have the power to understand, as all God's people should, how wide, how long, how high, and how deep his love is. May you experience the love of Christ, though it is too great to understand fully. Then you will be made complete with all the fullness of life and power that comes from God" (NLT).

Is there a more powerful phrase in the Bible than this one?

You are familiar with John 3:16, but do you know John 3:17, "God sent his Son into the world not to judge the world, but to save the world through him" (NLT). Christ did not come to punish the world – He came to save it! That's good news! No wonder Paul exclaims in Romans 1:16, "For I am not ashamed of this Good News about Christ. It is the power of God at work, saving everyone who believes—the Jew first and also the Gentile" (NLT).

The word "Gospel" means good news. We are to preach, to receive, to stand in, and be saved by the Gospel of Jesus Christ. A Restored Church teaches two parts to God's mysterious plan of love and grace:

(1) **Facts to be believed:** Paul defines the gospel in 1 Corinthians 15:3,4, "I passed on to you what was most important and what had also been passed on to me. Christ died for our sins, just as the Scriptures said. He was buried, and he was raised from the dead on the third day, just as the Scriptures said" (NLT).

These are the facts of the Gospel – the death, burial and resurrection of Jesus. In 1 Corinthians 1:18, Paul summarizes the good news as THE WORD OF THE CROSS. We preach Christ crucified (1 Corinthians 1:23)!

No matter how good someone is, Heaven will *never* be experienced until they believe the good news of Jesus Christ! There is no other way. Some refuse to believe the evidence – Jesus was on the earth for forty days and made ten personal appearances *after* the resurrection; He fulfilled over 300 prophecies in the Old Testament.

The apostles throughout the New Testament appealed to two areas of Christ's life to establish that He was The Messiah. One was the resurrection and the other was fulfilled messianic prophecy. The Old Testament, written over a 1,500-year period, contains several hundred references to the coming Messiah. All of those were fulfilled in Christ and they establish a solid confirmation of His credentials as The Messiah.

Jesus said, "I am the way, the truth, and the life. No one can come to the Father except through me" (John 14:6, NLT). The mysterious plan begins with believing these facts!

Feelings are often very deceptive. You can feel so exhilarated by lifting weights or shoveling snow and ten minutes later, be dead! Playing a hunch at the race track or in Las Vegas doesn't lead to riches. The fallacy of a "feeling" Christianity is that it draws truth out of feeling instead of feeling *out of truth*. Only twice in Acts is the feeling of new converts mentioned. Both times it is *after* the person becomes a Christian. The eunuch "went on his way rejoicing" (Acts 8:26-39, NLT) and the Philippian jailer "and his entire household rejoiced because they all believed in God" (Acts 16:25-34, NLT). There is a lot of difference between having an experience and then going to the Bible and justifying it, and receiving God's Word and accepting its truth, even when there is no special feeling attached to it! When you start with the Gospel, sensations of love and joy *always follow*! Obey the commands and grow!

> **(2) Promises to be enjoyed:** The Gospel offers many great promises that include forgiveness of every sin, the presence of God's Holy Spirit, and everlasting life! Acts 2:38 and 3:19 say virtually the same thing. Acts 5:32 adds: "We are witnesses of these things and so is the Holy Spirit, who is given by God to those who obey him" (NLT). God gives His Holy Spirit to those who obey Him. "And anyone who believes in God's Son has eternal life. Anyone who doesn't obey the Son will never experience eternal life but remains under God's angry judgment" (John 3:36, NLT). You don't receive eternal life when you die – the Christian has eternal life now!

Salvation is more than just "joining a church" (of some sort), participating in a religious ceremony (occasionally), being a good neighbor (more or less), and helping the less fortunate (to some extent). Salvation is not received by an experience in a closet or in your car or at a community meeting. Salvation is available when we believe the facts and obey the commands of Christ! Then we bask in the joy of the assurances of Christ! We receive the Gospel within the family of Christians.

The Greek word for power is "dunamis." The power of the Gospel is *dynamite*! Light the fuse and enjoy the explosion. Don't just believe – RECEIVE!

Notice Ephesians 3:17, again, "Your roots will grow down into God's love and keep you strong" (NLT).

When you grow down into God's love, that will keep you strong, and when God's love gets into you and you love other people with a Christ-like love, you will see before your very eyes, God restore His mysterious plan in somebody else's life.

I've known Doug and Debbie Gifford for over thirty years. Read the story of Doug and Debbie Gifford and how God's mysterious plan came to life! (Debbie attended that "new" class in 1987, but here is their story just recorded in an interview shown at our church in 2017.)

DOUG: Shortly after we were married, we started realizing we had many differences. I'd not been brought up in a Christian home, and shortly after we were married, Deb gave her life to Christ, and I wasn't against that in any way, but I guess the best thing to say is that I just wasn't all in. I didn't understand it, I didn't identify with it.

DEBBIE: We had a lot of challenges ... I had some illnesses, and they were chronic illnesses where I ended up in the hospital several times, and he was home ... taking care of the children and working. We had a lot of support from the church, the pastors, many church friends helped with meals, but it was a time where he didn't know what was wrong with me; we really didn't know how to deal with the whole thing. That was a pretty challenging time.

DOUG: After we got through that, I discovered I had cancer. Those were tough times. Not having the power to fix the things, not understanding why they were happening to me, not having the strength and the relationships and the faith to help me get through it.

DEBBIE: We were headed for divorce. We had separated, we had checked with attorneys, and that was the way it was going to be, and God just had different plans. He totally restored our marriage to something that we never thought we would ever have.

DOUG: I actually accepted the Lord Jesus as my Savior in 2008. But it was really after years of watching the Lord work through Debbie. I attended Bible studies and sometimes came to church, oftentimes didn't. I left her alone to do that, but I was open to it because I could see people with faith .... how they acted, how they dealt with things, how they treated other people. That involved a lot of Debbie's close friends, people we met through Bible studies and so forth, people here at church ... I just gradually softened.

DEBBIE: I prayed for Doug for thirty years, from about 1978 to 2008, when he gave his life to the Lord.

DOUG: It seemed like her faith gave her a power and a soft heart, and a joyful heart for helping others. It started working, it really did!

DEBBIE: We talk about that almost daily, about how the Lord worked in our marriage, and He's given us forty-four years that we didn't think we were going to have.

What if Debbie stopped praying after twenty-nine years? We will never know because she kept believing in God's mysterious plan.

ACTION STEPS FOR OUR STORY

1. Have you surrendered to His mysterious plan?
2. Is your church a work of Restoration in progress?
3. What, how, and when is your church going to celebrate?

JESUS' THIRD PRIORITY: EVANGELISM

God has a plan for you and me and, if we peek around that corner, we see that God has a plan for every person who has ever lived, who will ever live, and who is currently living.

That means that the neighbor who openly denies the existence of God is still living in the shadow of a Kingdom purpose, with significance and true fulfillment within reach but just beyond his immediate view and experience. The Muslim, the Hindu, the Jehovah's Witness, and followers of every other religion have access to living water that can forever quench their thirst but are living unaware and absent of their good fortune.

God desires that every tongue, tribe, and nation be called among his people, a truth easily discerned through a study of Jesus. He redefined what it means to be a neighbor. He fraternized with the dregs of society. Jesus freely offered compassion, love, peace, and salvation to anyone regardless of their individual circumstance, belief system, or social status. He died a criminal's death to cover our sin debt – but also the sin debt of anyone else who accepts Him as Lord and Savior.

In this truth lies the heart and power of the Great Commission. He commanded his followers to follow His example, to go make disciples, to baptize, and to teach anyone and everyone who will listen. On the flip side, Jesus is communicating that it is critical for Christians to fight the temptation to wallow in the satisfaction, confidence, and complacency of one's salvation.

God's plan for saving the world – His only plan for the world - is for the Church, manifested in the individual believers of which it is comprised, to cast a bright light into the darkness and share the Gospel with those who are yet far off, separated from a God who desperately want all people to come to a knowledge of His truth, love, and grace.

CHAPTER FOUR

RESTORED LIFE

Restored Lives are restored by restored lives! As I reflect on how *God* restored my brokenness, I now understand that He expects me to live so that others can be restored as well.

RESTORING ME

I've asked myself, what if I was never given the opportunity to speak in Junior Church when I was a kid? What if I never was asked to preach at campfire in high school when I was at church camp? What if my preacher never encouraged me to enter the full-time ministry?

Even though I *did* have a mother who supported my decision to be a preacher, in my opinion, it is unlikely that I would be a preacher today without the influence of my preacher.

During my teen years, my preacher, Max Hickerson, took me, along with his son, to ball games, and lots of church leaders' conferences. God used those experiences to show me two things: God uses ordinary people. My preacher taught me that it was OK to boo the umpire. (He was real.) But he also exposed me to the joy of working in God's kingdom! He taught me how to do life!

Here's the question for you: If you find yourself in the position of influencing those who are looking to you, are you *reproducing* yourself through your authentic, committed, and restored life?

Paul said to the young preacher, Timothy, "…entrust to reliable men who will also be qualified to teach others" (2 Timothy 2:2, NIV). ARE YOU DETERMINED TO DO JUST THAT?

In the first three chapters of Ephesians, the apostle Paul wrote to the First Century Ephesian Church how the Lord has restored our *identity*, our *unity*, and His *plan*.

But there is a significant shift in chapters 4, 5, 6: In light of what He has done, how should we *live*? What do "Restored" people and churches look like?

A New England Patriots fan had a lousy seat at the game. But he spotted an open seat on the fifty-yard line. So … he made his way to the empty seat, right behind the Patriots' bench.

When he got seated, he asked the guy beside him, "Is this seat taken?" "No, that was my wife's seat. She passed away." The fella said, "I'm so sorry about your loss. May I ask why you didn't give the ticket to a friend or relative?"

"Oh no," he said, "They're all at her funeral!"

We refer to them as fans because they are "fanatics" … to a fault! (*Especially* Patriots' fans!) Now, while sports are a good diversion, from the chaos of this world, that is not all there is to life. (In fact, a good job, decent wage, nice home, time to enjoy life and family and vacations and … "retirement," from the pressure, are all nice things. But, a "Restored Life" is so much more.

Ephesians 5:15-17 reads, "Be careful how you live. Don't live like fools, but like those who are wise. Make the most of every opportunity in these evil days. Don't act thoughtlessly, but understand what the Lord wants you to do" (NLT).

We will discuss our eternal life, later in this chapter, … but a Restored Life doesn't *just* refer to life after death … our lives should be restored, renewed, and refocused, *here and now*.

THE WAY WE VALUE WORTH

Every day, we hear of violence in the streets and in our homes, office workers who take home supplies: staples, calculators, computer diskettes. There's the guy who rewrites the figures of his income on his tax return.

But when people live by the world's value system, others get hurt, relationships die, and God's heart breaks. So ... a Restored Life finds value in three practical ways.

The way we see work

Ephesians 4:28, "If you are a thief, quit stealing" (NLT).

I know we have a love-hate relationship with work. Have you heard the adage: "Early to bed and early to rise, makes a man healthy, wealthy and wise!" But did you know there's a second verse? "But what does it matter how much he wins, if he's always asleep when the fun begins."

If you are a workaholic: Pay attention! Work can exercise our bodies and minds. In fact, Paul told the Corinthian believers to take care of their bodies. And work can change our environment. Building, planning, and accomplishing meaningful jobs provide a good balance to just sitting around, doing nothing. Work can foster God-given creativity. Remember Adam and Eve were placed in the Garden "to take care of it." God not only gives gardens, but we can take the raw materials of God's creation, and turn it into the stuff of culture and civilization, in the city.

And work provides a way to "earn" a living. So, we can provide for our family's needs.

As Restored believers, even work can take on new meaning! A Restored Life changes...

The way we manage wealth

Ephesians 4:28, "Use your hands for good hard work, and then give generously to others in need" (NLT).

Paul encourages capitalism. Earning money and having an income is a good thing. Wealth, in of itself, is not wrong. Some of the greatest followers of the Lord in Scripture were wealthy. *Solomon*: Richest ever. *Abraham*: Wealthy in cattle. *Job*: Had more than he could spend. *Joseph of Arimathea's* wealth allowed Jesus' body to have a resting place (for three days)! *Barnabas* was wealthy, but he used it to feed the poor.

In the Parable of the Three Servants, Jesus said one of them buried the wealth he'd been given in the ground. But the master said, "At least you could have put it in the bank to earn interest."

Wealth is a way of expanding the treasures God has given.

I enjoyed reading about a bride-to-be, in July 2017, who was getting ready to marry, when she suddenly had to call off the wedding. The couple had spent lots of money on a party. The bride called everyone, canceled, apologized, cried, called vendors, cried some more, and then started feeling really sick about just throwing away all the food ordered for the reception.

After discussing it with her ex-groom, they both decided to use the cancellation as an *opportunity* to help people in *need*. She called homeless shelters in Indianapolis and invited them to a special reception dinner.

She turned a painful experience into a joyful one for families in need.

As Restored people of God, our ability to earn a good living is a *new way* to care for *others*, and provide *funds* for the ministry of God!

A Restored Life also impacts …

The way we give generously

God expects His people to share. If you are a Restored son or daughter of God, make it a habit to give away a portion of the money and time loaned to you by God.

The most profound sense of grace in a person's life is generosity.

Malachi 3:10, "'Bring all the tithes into the storehouse so there will be enough food in my Temple. If you do,' (says the LORD), 'I will open the windows of Heaven for you. I will pour out a blessing so great you won't have enough room to take it in! Try it! Put me to the test!'" (NLT)

Did you know that a person can fake everything about the Christian life *except* generosity?

RESTORING THE CHURCH

I had the privilege of seeing how the generosity of Restored Lives can glorify God. In September 2013, Connection Pointe Christian Church launched a campaign we called *Unstoppable,* based on Acts 4:20, "We cannot stop telling about everything we have seen and heard" (NLT). The people committed to give $15 million toward expanding our facility for projected growth. $7 million, over and above the committed amount, was given! A two-year total of $22 million! Kid City was built for our children, another worship venue was added which seats 500 people, as well as a new entrance for our Fitness Center, and the former chapel was remodeled into a Student Center, where 400 students now worship every week.

Why did the Connection Pointe Family give? It came from a heart of compassion and that mindset is rooted in our relationship with God and others. When we believe that *everything* we have comes from God and He takes care of those who are generous with the church and others, God multiplies our gifts as we place them in His hands.

When a generous attitude leads to generosity, we learn that one of the greatest blessings we are given is being able to bless others. And ... when we bless others, He blesses us.

Psalm 112:5 says, "Good comes to those who lend money generously and conduct their business fairly" (NLT).

Proverbs 11:25, "The generous will prosper; those who refresh others will themselves be refreshed" (NLT).

In July 2016, my wife and I were driving to Asheville, NC (the worst storm you can imagine for two hours, in the Smoky Mountains). We checked into our room, grabbed a bite to eat. I brought Kristen to the door, to drop her off ... it was pouring and lightning. A car pulled in front of us ... A woman got out and said, "Please, Mister, I'm out of gas ..." I said, "Follow us." We offered to fill it up. She said, "No, ten gallons will be fine." Then she said, "Thank you so much. I just have to trust in Jesus. I asked Him to send an angel ..." (I pointed to my wife.) ... Then she said, "What's your name, so I can thank God for you tonight?" I said, "Steve, Pastor Steve and Kristen!"

She started to cry ... so I asked Lisa if I could pray for her right then ...

Here's the question ... Who do you think was more "refreshed"? Lisa or us? Our Father blesses those who will bless others!

By the way, that story had nothing to do with me. I was only generous because "my angel," my wife, was watching me!

Would you read carefully this letter I received from a church member in 2017. She wrote:

> *I actually wrote this in May, but was not sure that I should send it until we got our cards back in the mail and both mine and Kurt's*

said, *"Tithe on Gross Income."* Then I was sure we needed to share our story.

We had been tithing on our net income for years, but this year when you said, *"Do you want God to bless your gross income or your net income?"* Our hearts began to change about our tithing amount. *(In February, we increased our online giving amount to cover our gross income.)*

Please be aware that our car had over 200,000 miles on it, we were literally holding our washing machine together with duct tape, the oven quit working right, and then to top it off, a medical bill of $6,000 was not covered by insurance! *(But, God says, "Test me in this." We did not change our online giving amount from our February decision.)*

(So, this is what God does ...) Several years ago, Kurt made an investment of $82 into the company he works for. In a recent move by the company to reorganize its stocks, Kurt was offered over $300,000 for PART of his stock investment, and starting monthly, we would receive over $6,000 per month for the next five years! Not done yet ... this year our tax return was $20,000! *(Not done yet)* ... the company set this stock payback up so that we would not be responsible for the tax on the whole amount now, but over the five-year period. *(Then the company gives us the money to cover the taxes.)*

Our investment advisor said that this was the best scenario he has *EVER HEARD!*

Kurt and I know this is straight from Malachi 3:10, "Bring the WHOLE tithe ... and see if I will not throw open the floodgates of Heaven and pour out so much blessing that you will not have room for it."

Luke 6:38, "Give, and you will receive. Your gift will return to you in full—pressed down, shaken together to make room for more, running over, and poured into your lap. The amount you give will determine the amount you get back" (NLT).

A Restored Life's *work* becomes new and a Restored Life's *words* become new.

THE WAY WE USE WORDS

Notice three commands concerning our words:

Be honest

Ephesians 4:25-26, "Stop telling lies. Let us tell our neighbors the truth, for we are all parts of the same body. And 'don't sin by letting anger control you'" (NLT).

We are *expected* to speak the truth. Now, we *are* tempted to not speak the truth when we are angry at someone ... to make *us* look better and them look worse. So ... when you speak ... be honest.

Be helpful

Ephesians 4:29, "... Let everything you say be good and helpful, so that your words will be an encouragement to those who hear them" (NLT).

Get rid of abusive language. Verbal abuse can be just as damaging as physical abuse.

Have you ever looked forward to eating a piece of fruit, but when you bit into it, it was rotten? That's the word Paul uses here.

So, don't speak rotten words, but do say words that are helpful and encouraging. But then he says, in verse 30, "Do not bring sorrow to God's Holy Spirit by the way you live...." (NLT). If *you* have been restored by God, only say words that *refresh* others!

Be kind

Ephesians 4:31-32, "Get rid of all bitterness, rage, anger, harsh words, and slander, as well as all types of evil behavior. Instead, be kind to each other, tenderhearted, forgiving one another, just as God through Christ has forgiven you" (NLT).

Pretty straightforward words and easy to obey, right? Wrong. It is a battle!

ACTION STEPS FOR OUR STORY

Ephesians 4:21-22, "Since you have heard about Jesus and have learned the truth that comes from him, throw off your old sinful nature and your former way of life ..." (NLT).

What did you used to do or say, that do you do not do now, since God is restoring you? Maybe you used to "fit" church into your schedule, if it didn't conflict with something more important (like spending weekends doing things that kept you away from church on the weekend). Not necessarily bad things, just not the *best* things.

One guy said to a friend, "You look depressed. What are you thinking about?" ... "My future." ... "What makes your future look so hopeless?" ... "My past."

You see ... a Restored Life *doesn't* obsess over looking *back* at past sins/ brokenness ... Because ...

You cannot dwell on the past if you want to make progress in the future.

Is there a part of your past that still hangs on? Is there something you once did, that still troubles you?

1. Intentionally overcome the past.

Romans 8:12-14, "Dear brothers and sisters, you have no obligation to do what your sinful nature urges you to do. For if you live by its dictates, you will die. But if through the power of the Spirit you put to death the deeds of your sinful nature, you will live. For all who are led by the Spirit of God are children of God" (NLT).

Get in His Word, talk to Him in prayer, find a way to serve Him and others.

The more we do for the Lord, the less we are tempted by the sinful nature. In fact, Connection Pointe Christian Church has impacted our community to such a degree that our community would definitely notice if the life and light of the Connection Pointe Family went out!

Here's just a sampling of the impact Connection Pointe has had on many lives!

Community support for under-resourced families

- Worked with school district to identify 230 families (845 children) to support throughout the Christmas season.
- Each child received a winter coat, hat and gloves, three toys, complete outfit, pajamas, underwear and socks, shoes selected by the parents at a Christmas event at the church.
- Each family had a host assigned to them that built a relationship with them and came to each Christmas event. Many of these relationships have continued and families have accepted Christ and joined Connection Pointe as a result of the "The Christmas Project."
- The parents participated by paying a very small amount for these items that created a "partnership" and ownership from the parents. This gave them respect and dignity as well. The money raised was given to our local homeless partner.

Partnered with Clarence Farrington Elementary School

- Project Classroom – Each teacher (seventy) shared five items they wanted for their classroom, these were items that they would normally have to pay out of pocket. Church members purchased the items and they were presented to the teachers at a "red carpet event" held in their honor. Items amounted to over a total of $102,000 in in-kind donations.
- The Clarence Farrington Community Center. This is evening programing for adults and students at Clarence Farrington Elementary School that is funded and led by Connection Pointe staff and volunteers. Each week there are over 320 adults and students who participate and 120 who volunteer. Programming includes ESL for adults, GED for adults, budgeting and Parenting classes, food pantry, student tutoring, martial arts, dance, 4-H, boy scouts and girl scouts. Every Wednesday evening is family night where families come together for a free meal and fun. This is a great relational opportunity!

PIE day

■ Every year on March 14 we deliver a homemade pie to over 600 teachers in our community, thanking them for their contribution to our community. Each pie is made by members of Connection Pointe.

Salvation Army

■ We have a strong relationship with the Salvation Army Rehabilitation Center for men who are participating in the drug & alcohol rehabilitation program.

■ One on one counseling by church members at the center takes place weekly by volunteer retired pastors and counselors at Connection Pointe.

■ Men come out for dinner and games six times a year. In the last two years, 127 men have accepted Christ and been baptized through this partnership, on our Baptism Weekends at Connection Pointe Christian Church.

Allow God to grip your heart as you read these two of hundreds of stories I could share.

MY CHRISTMAS PROJECT EXPERIENCE

I went through a divorce in 2011. I was solely responsible for four children under the age of thirteen, and I did not know how I was going to supply their day-to-day needs. Someone anonymously submitted my name for The Christmas Project in 2013. I was completely overwhelmed, humbled and blessed by the outpouring of love, support, care and compassion we received. I continued to be a recipient of the program for two more years after that, each time having the same feelings of relief that my kids were going to be happy for the holidays.

Last year I received a huge blessing from the Lord and was promoted at work, which then allowed me to be able to fully handle my finances alone. I decided it was time to start giving back!

Being a former recipient and now a family host in The Christmas Project, I know the impact it makes on the families involved. And as a host, I am glad I can share my story and encourage other families with our experience. We are blessed to have the opportunity to pay it forward and continue to spread His Word and love for others.

MY EXPERIENCE WITH THE CHRISTMAS PROJECT

Raising my grandsons is not where I thought my life would be at this time. I found out about Connection Pointe through my grandson's school, five years ago when he started kindergarten. The school social worker told me about a program at Connection Pointe that could help with Christmas, which I was eternally grateful for. While being a part of The Neighborhood (now known as The Christmas Project), I was able to meet other church members and decided to check out a church service.

Connection Pointe has been wonderful for my family in many ways and provided year-round support. Everyone that I have met here has given me encouragement, warmth and love ... even people who do not know me or my story.

Without The Christmas Project I think I would still be lost. I have found the path, I see the path and now I just need to touch and walk the path ... and not be scared. The Community Impact Team has told me that I do not walk alone, and I am so very happy to be a part of the Connection Pointe Family.

Regardless of the size or location of your church, your congregation and community would be changed if you just put a plan like this in place right now!

Ephesians 4:23-24, "Let the Spirit renew your thoughts and attitudes. Put on your new nature, created to be like God—truly righteous and holy" (NLT).

We are better *in* Christ than we are without Him! Have you ever had someone say to you, "You really clean up nice!" (Most people look better "cleaned up," don't we?)

But we're talking about *inner* cleanliness. We also look better to God when we've been cleansed from sin ... So, put on your new nature!

1. Deliberately, put on the new nature.
    (1) Imitate others.
        1 Corinthians 11:1, "Follow my example, as I follow the example of Christ" (NIV).
        Find somebody who is following Christ and follow them! Better yet ...
    (2) Focus on Jesus.
        Hebrews 12:1 says, "... let us strip off every weight that slows us down, especially the sin that so easily trips us up. And let us run with endurance the race God has set before us" (NLT).
        Verse 2, "We do this by keeping our eyes on Jesus ..."
        Why? The more we keep our eyes on Jesus, the more we will eventually become more like Him!

2. Absolutely give no opportunity to the devil.

The English Standard Version translates Ephesians 4:26-27, "Be angry and do not sin; do not let the sun go down on your anger, and give no opportunity to the devil" (ESV).

Have you ever been in a hurry and the car in front of you stops at a yellow light? I heard about a guy who was furious, honking his horn, screaming at the car who stopped on yellow.

The guy in the car behind was still in mid-rant, and there was a tap on the window. It was a police officer. He ordered the fella out of the car ... took him to the police station where he was searched, fingerprinted, photographed, and placed in a holding cell.

A couple hours later, a police officer opened the door of the cell and told the man he was free to go. "I'm sorry. I made a mistake. You see, when I saw you blowing your horn, flipping off the person in front of you, I noticed your 'Jesus Is My Co-Pilot' sticker and your 'Choose Life' license plate holder, so I assumed you had stolen the car!"

Whether we realize it or not, we give the devil an opportunity, when we don't act like or speak like a follower of Christ.

How can we take away that opportunity from Satan?

James 4:7-8 says, "Humble yourselves before God. Resist the devil, and he will flee from you. Come close to God, and God will come close to you" (NLT).

The only way to throw off the sinful nature, put on the new nature, not give Satan an opportunity, is by humbling and surrendering ourselves to God!

Colossians 2:6,12, "Just as you accepted Christ Jesus as your Lord, you must continue to follow him. ... For you were buried with Christ when you were baptized. And with him you were raised to new life because you trusted the mighty power of God, who raised Christ from the dead" (NLT).

Baptism is how you demonstrate that you have died to your old self by being crucified with Christ. Immersion in water is a beautiful picture of burying the past.

When we are generous with God's money and kind with our words, it not only reflects *our* "Restored Life" but it leads to new life and the celebration of new lives through Bible baptisms.

We have seen over 5,200 people immersed into Christ, in the last thirty-one years, but when Ben Katz, a lifelong Jewish man, was baptized on a Sunday morning, it changed our church. Read his words and you'll see why:

I first started attending Brownsburg Christian Church in early 1995. I was in a relationship and ended up marrying a lady who was a strong Christian lady and I would come with her as a guest. Although I was not raised as a Christian, I was very open to her beliefs. I was raised in a conservative Jewish home, and considered myself Jewish, and was satisfied with that situation. I enjoyed coming to Brownsburg Christian, and then Connection Pointe. It was a very friendly, very open, very tolerant church, and I really enjoyed listening to the various sermons.

At times, I had questions and I would talk to people and get the answer ... sometimes I agreed, and sometimes I didn't agree, but I was always treated with respect, and over the years, it just started to make sense to me. It started to maybe fill a void that I didn't know was there. I accepted Christ and was baptized in August 2013. I don't remember there being one specific instance or specific discussion or specific happening that changed my mind or made me want to follow Christ and become a Christian, but it was mainly Pastor Reeves that helped me with my journey.

I think it's important for a non-Christian who is attending a Christian church, to be treated with understanding, and that people oftentimes, even not knowing it, are open to discussions with those beliefs. One Sunday service, there were some people sitting in front of me, a young lady turned around and we introduced each other, and she just openly said, "So, what's your story?" I briefly told her my story, and that type of interest in a total stranger was very welcoming, and I think it's important for the church to be a welcoming, warm location and Connection Pointe has been that warm, open, welcoming environment for me.

JESUS' FOURTH PRIORITY: DISCIPLESHIP

One of the most common themes in Jesus' ministry is life change in the people He encounters. He told the rich young ruler to sell everything. He told the woman caught in adultery to go and sin no more. He told the lame man to get up, pick up his mat, and go home. He even told the crowd to hate their own father, mother, wife, children, brothers, and sisters. Others such as Zaccheus were innately compelled to change as a result of crossing paths with Jesus.

The life changes in some cases appeared to be strictly physical but in every case the transformation reflected some measure of spiritual growth – some manifestation of faith in action toward a clearer reflection of God. Jesus' emphasis on growth foreshadowed the role of the Church as a transformational community.

The *Ekklesia* is by nature being "called out" from the world, to be a holy people that constantly strives to reflect Christ more and more every day. This requires the Church, consisting of individual believers, to pursue relationships marked by support, accountability, and encouragement toward an ever greater alignment with Jesus. It requires a constant struggle against the enemy inside ourselves – that manifests in pride, sinful desire, and selfishness – as well as the enemy, Satan, who prowls around like a lion looking for someone to devour.

It requires His people to think differently, act differently, and interact differently – differently from the world but also differently than they did yesterday. It compels Christians to live more generously, to serve more selflessly, and to share their faith more boldly as they continue to better understand what it means to be a disciple of Christ.

Ephesians 4:21,23,24,29, "Since you have heard about Jesus and have learned the truth that comes from him … Instead, let the Spirit renew your thoughts and attitudes. Put on your new nature … Let everything you say be good and helpful, so that your words will be an encouragement to those who hear them" (NLT).

CHAPTER FIVE

RESTORED WISDOM

I am writing this book, just after forty years of full-time pastoral ministry. You would think that qualifies me to be in the "sage phase." My pastor, Max Hickerson, sent these to me, when I turned sixty:

Q: Why should 60-plus year-old people use valet parking?
A: Valets don't forget where they park your car.

Q: Is it common for 60-plus year-olds to have problems with short-term memory storage?
A: Storing memory is not a problem, retrieving it is the problem.

Q: As people age, do they sleep more soundly?
A: Yes, but usually in the afternoon.

Q: Where should 60-plus year-olds look for eyeglasses?
A: On their foreheads.

Q: What is the most common remark made by 60-plus year-olds when they enter antique stores?
A: "Gosh, I remember these!"

However, sixty years of life and forty years of pastoral ministry do *not* automatically qualify anyone to be declared wise. Ephesians 5:15-16 reads, "So be careful how you live. Don't live like fools, but like those who are wise. Make the most of every opportunity in these evil days" (NLT).

Since I'm over sixty, here's some honesty: Ephesians 5:1 reads, "Imitate God, therefore, in everything you do, because you are his dear children" (NLT).

Imitate God! That is pretty clear!! No matter how much experience, we are *still works* of Restoration ... *in Progress*.

A young pastor was asked by a funeral director to conduct a graveside service for a homeless man. (He had no family or friends.) I have personally done that before and it breaks your heart.

This cemetery was out in the country, but it was new and this man's body was to be the first one laid to rest there. This was before GPS and the young pastor got lost and got there an hour late.

The backhoe, the excavating digger, was there, the crew was eating their lunch, but the hearse was nowhere in sight.

The pastor apologized for being late, but as he looked into the open grave, the vault lid was already in place. He told them it wouldn't take long, but he needed to do what was proper. So ... the workers, still eating their lunch, gathered around.

That young pastor poured out his heart! He started preachin'! The workers got involved: "Amen!" Preach it! Praise the Lord!" The young pastor really got fired up now ... He preached from Genesis to Revelation!

Finally, when the service was over, he walked over to his car. As he opened the door, one of the workers yelled, "Pastor, I have never seen anything like that before ... in twenty years of putting in septic systems!"

Young pastors and older pastors need wisdom! It'll save us from embarrassment, *if* that wisdom is from above!

I received this letter a few weeks ago, from a young man in our church. He wrote:

"Friday, I was leaving work and God was really tugging at my heart to go be with some old friends and their mom... she was diagnosed with lung cancer. She was only in her early fifties. I'm driving down Interstate-74, thinking I'm going home but God's voice was really prevalent. I knew they were in Danville, somewhere, but not real sure *where*. I drove around until I found the nursing home. They were surprised to see me. At first I thought 'What am I doing here? What am I going to say?' I walked into their hospice room and both of them said, *'How did you know that we needed you? How did you even know where we were?'* I told them that God had tugged at me to come be with them and that I wanted to pray for them and their mom.

I spent about two hours with them. Sharing *what God had done in my life* over the past couple of years and *letting them know that HE was there for them as well.* At the end of our visit, I prayed with them. They asked if I would pray over their mom and I did. When I started to pray and let her know that Jesus loved *her*, she started to try to open her eyes and started squeezing the girls' hands. (She was unresponsive for the last day or so.) I realized that God was using me to help lead them to HIM.

Let's move on to church Saturday night. I was sitting there with a heavy heart for them, and then you read about the *first day in Heaven.* I closed my eyes and God gives me this vision of her (their mom), she was beautiful. Blond wavy hair. She was standing among the crowd of people praising God. I didn't want to open my eyes. *I then prayed.* 'God, if they need anything, anything at all, please have them reach out to me. I will be YOUR hands and feet.'

As soon as I said that prayer, my phone goes off. Four times! The text said: 'Could you please come back here and be with us!' I told the family when we left what had happened. I said, 'God is calling me to go up and be with this family.' I went up and after about two hours of being with them. Their mom took her last breath. I shared with them the vision God had given me when you were talking about our first day in Heaven. A great peace came over everyone in the room."

My friend, Justin, concluded with these words:

> "Your message on that night and then to see someone go to Heaven that *same night.* And for me to be reaching out to some people I haven't really been around for quite some time.
>
> They now have asked me to officiate their mom's funeral. I don't even know what this means...but I know that *God will guide me* every step of the way."

That young man is wise.

RESTORING ME

Wisdom is not just what we know, it is how we live. Here are four practical words of advice, from God's Word, that will help every one of us, as God continues His work of restoration in us, regardless of our age.

Make careful choices

Ephesians 5:15, "Be careful how you live. Don't live like fools, but like those who are wise" (NLT).

This is a command: Be careful! Has anybody learned, the hard way, to walk very carefully in the dark? But when it's dark, you not only need to walk carefully, but you need the light of a cell phone to walk carefully and wisely.

Ephesians 5:8-14, "Once you were full of darkness, but now you have light from the Lord. So live as people of light! For this light within you produces only what is good and right and true. Carefully determine what pleases the Lord. Take no part in the worthless deeds of evil and darkness; instead, expose them. It is shameful even to talk about the things that ungodly people do in secret. But their evil intentions will be exposed when the light shines on them, for the light makes everything visible. This is why it is said, 'Awake, O sleeper, rise up from the dead, and Christ will give you light'" (NLT).

The darkness is exposed, when you turn on the light. How *do* we see in the darkness of the world, so we can make wise, careful choices? It is when we become *restored*, people of light!

We must let it show us *where* to walk and where to *not* walk ... wherever we go!

The late Dwight L. Moody told about a terrible accident in which several students were killed when their car was hit by a train. At the trial, they questioned the watchman, who had the job of waving a lantern to warn of danger. He was asked, "Were you at the crossing that night?" "Yes, your Honor." "Were you waving your lantern?" "Yes, your Honor, but the light had gone out."

Jesus said in Matthew 5:14-16, "You are the light of the world—like a city on a hilltop that cannot be hidden. No one lights a lamp and then puts it under a basket. Instead, a lamp is placed on a stand, where it gives light to everyone in the house. In the same way, let your good deeds shine out for all to see, so that everyone will praise your heavenly Father" (NLT).

How *do* we let our light shine? By making careful, godly choices, based on God's Word. And notice, it didn't say to "speak up" for the Lord. Do you know why? Have you ever heard of the game, *Show & Tell*? If you are not making godly choices or living a wise life, please don't tell them about your Jesus. Because until you can *show* the light, you have no business *telling* about the light!

Jesus said in John 8:12, "I am the light of the world. If you follow me, you won't have to walk in darkness, because you will have the light that leads to life" (NLT).

We are not perfect, of course! But make sure you are making progress by following Him! As Paul said in 1 Corinthians 11:1, "Follow my example, as I follow the example of Christ" (NIV).

Someone wrote: "Waste your money and you're only out of money. Waste your life and you've lost a part of your life."

(I like this one): "Don't count every hour, make every hour count!" That's tweetable!

Just how important are our choices?

Ephesians 5:16 says, "Make the most of every opportunity in these evil days" (NLT). This sounds urgent ... TIME WILL RUN OUT. (It may have already run out for some people, because they've continued to rebel against God.)

First Thessalonians 5:3 says, "When people are saying, 'Everything is peaceful and secure,' then disaster will fall on them as suddenly as a pregnant woman's labor pains begin. And there will be no escape" (NLT).

When is that time going to happen? It could be any time. The apostle Paul wrote in 2 Timothy 4:6, "... my life has already been poured out as an offering to God. The time of my death is near" (NLT).

What about you? Is the time of your death near?

Somebody said, "Yesterday is a canceled check, tomorrow is a promissory note; today is the only cash you have ..." Spend it wisely ... one choice at a time!

Cultivate healthy emotions

Notice Ephesians 5:18, "Don't be drunk with wine, because that will ruin your life. Instead, be filled with the Holy Spirit" (NLT).

What a contrast: "*Don't* get drunk ... *Do* be filled with the Holy Spirit."

People talk about "keeping my emotions under control" (That is *not* how it works.) You *surrender* your mind, heart and emotions to *His* control! What does that look like?

Galatians 5:22-23, "The Holy Spirit produces this kind of fruit in our lives: love, joy, peace, patience, kindness, goodness, faithfulness, gentleness, and self-control" (NLT).

Romans 8:9 reads, (if you've surrendered to Christ), "You are not controlled by your sinful nature. You are controlled by the Spirit if you have the Spirit of God living in you. (And remember that those who do not have the Spirit of Christ living in them do not belong to him at all)" (NLT).

Romans 8:12-14, "Therefore, dear brothers and sisters, you have no obligation to do what your sinful nature urges you to do. For if you live by its dictates, you will die. But if through the power of the Spirit you put to death the deeds of your sinful nature, you will live. For all who are led by the Spirit of God are children of God" (NLT).

What does that mean? It means to be sensitive to His Spirit, inside of us. Respond to His promptings!

And the clearest way to do that is to read His Word and walk with the Lord, in constant prayer. Here's more wisdom:

Maintain a joyful attitude

Ephesians 5:19 speaks of "... singing psalms and hymns and spiritual songs among yourselves, and making music to the Lord in your hearts" (NLT).

This is why God instructed the Church to come together, at least every week, to share the inner trust we have in God (joy) with others. Connection Pointe Christian Church has a "Culture of Joy." That is more than laughter, but laughter is a part of it. ... it encourages others and reminds us to keep our eyes on Him, even when the circumstances of life are not going so well. When life hurts, laughter and joy really help! Proverbs 17:22, "A cheerful heart is good medicine, but a broken spirit saps a person's strength" (NLT).

Music lifts the soul and the emotions. So, healthy, restored churches laugh a lot, and sing a lot! What do we sing?

(1) *Psalms*: The Old Testament book is the source of many of the songs we sing *directly* to God.

(2) *Hymns*: They exalt the *character* of God.

(3) *Spiritual Songs*: They remind us of how God has and is restoring our souls, by His grace and mercy!

When we sing psalms, hymns and spiritual songs to the Lord, a joy wells up within us, as our words reflect His Spirit in our hearts, and keep our focus on the Lord, instead of the pain of this world! Many people visit a church as a guest, and they are drawn to come back: Lots of different reasons ... one of them is that they feel a spirit of *joy*, and for some people, their life is so painful, the *only* time in their week when they hear laughter is when they come to church, each weekend, and leave with a cheerful heart.

Here's one more word of wisdom...

Express genuine gratitude

Ephesians 5:20, "Give thanks for everything to God the Father in the name of our Lord Jesus Christ" (NLT).

When things are good, it's easy to be thankful. But gratitude, when times are difficult, is the real deal. It's authentic! It's genuine! But you won't drift into this habit ... you will need to intentionally make the wise choice to be joyful and grateful!

The apostle Paul wrote from a prison cell, where he'd been placed because of telling others about Jesus in Philippians 4:4,6,7, "Always be full of joy in the Lord. I say it again—rejoice! Don't worry about anything; instead, pray about everything. Tell God what you need, and thank him for all he has done. Then you will experience God's peace, which exceeds anything we can understand. His peace will guard your hearts and minds as you live in Christ Jesus" (NLT).

So ... "give thanks for everything ..." ... and "...pray about everything

…" Then … "His peace will guard your hearts and minds as you live (wisely) in Jesus Christ" (Philippians 4:6-7).

Question: Are you growing in wisdom? Are you growing in the *Lord's* wisdom? The only place to find that is in "The Ancient Book."

Deuteronomy 4:2, "Do not add to or subtract from these commands I am giving you. Just obey the commands of the LORD your God that I am giving you" (NLT).

Revelation 22:18-19, "And I solemnly declare to everyone who hears the words of prophecy written in this book: If anyone adds anything to what is written here, God will add to that person the plagues described in this book. And if anyone removes any of the words from this book of prophecy, God will remove that person's share in the tree of life and in the holy city that are described in this book" (NLT).

This is what it means to be a Restored Church. God's Word rules!

RESTORING THE CHURCH

Tampering with divine revelation is dealt with in the early pages of the Old Testament and in the last chapter of the New Testament. In both cases, it is strictly *prohibited*. Sacred scripture needs no alterations, either by addition or subtraction. No updating needs to be done, for the faith was delivered … ONCE FOR ALL … (Jude 3).

As we recall the early days of the Restoration Movement, Thomas Campbell was a preacher in the Presbyterian Church in Washington, Pennsylvania. Many came to hear Campbell. A group of traveling Baptists were present on Communion Sunday. He invited them to participate in the Lord's Supper. This, along with other departures from the rules, led to charges being filed against him. He was later suspended from ministerial office by the Synod.

In 1809, Thomas Campbell wrote the "Declaration and Address." It proposes to lessen the authority of human thought and opinion and return to the authority of Christ and His Divine Word! Alexander Campbell, in 1836, listed among seven essentials for a restoration of the church "a more intimate, general and special acquaintance with the holy oracles of both Testaments." Take the Bible alone as our sole written authority!

A man wanted to make a demonstration to his sons. He handed them a bundle of sticks, and told each to break them. All tried, only to fail. He then took the bundle apart and broke them one at a time saying, "In unity there is strength." The individual members of the church must have something to bind them together. There can be no unity without authority. There can be no knowledge without some way to convey that knowledge. Jesus possessed *all* authority in heaven and earth, stating that the Scriptures testified of Him. We cannot have faith in Him without knowing something *of* Him. Our *only* original source of information is the Bible. The Word of God is the only charter for the church today. The Bible only, makes Christians only.

A Restored Church understands that a *unity* in Christ takes place by testing all beliefs and practices on the basis of the Bible. Division is often caused by the mixture of human opinion with God's revelation.

Christianity is primarily a *Person* to receive, not a set of *rules* to believe. Growing in Christ means growing in *wisdom*. As a tool becomes sharpened by being pressed against the stone, so minds become wiser when pressed against the Word of God.

However, the right ideas *about* the Word of God are *not* the same as *knowing* The Book itself. Second Timothy 3:16-17 says, "All Scripture is inspired by God and is useful to teach us what is true and to make us realize what is wrong in our lives. It corrects us when we are wrong and teaches us to do what is right. God uses it to prepare and equip his people to do every good work" (NLT).

At Connection Pointe Christian Church, we recently interviewed one of the wisest people I know. She has been an encouragement to my wife and me, as well as hundreds of others. Even though this season of life is difficult, listen to the wisdom of our friend, Sue Farmer, from the Connection Pointe Family:

I like to quote the Scripture from Psalm 19:14, "Let the words of my mouth and the meditations of my heart be acceptable unto You, O Lord, my Strength and my Redeemer."

I've had some traumatic things happen in my life, like many, many people, and I know without a doubt, that without Him with me, there's no way I could have gotten through the situations I've been in. I've lost two husbands, both wonderful men. Particularly, people here know Gib, and he was an inspiration to me. I think there's a difference between happiness and joy.

Sometimes we tend to blend the two, and to me, I think being joyful is praising Him and being grateful for what He's giving me, because I'm so blessed in so many ways – with relationships I have with others, with my family, with my church. I went through, and of course, still go through the grieving period, as I'm sure I always will. But I'm trying to reach out now, to where I can serve, to help that grief, but put it behind me as much as possible. So, if I reach out to others, then I think I can maintain a happier attitude at helping someone else.

I'm a big believer in prayer, that it's very essential, so that helps me with decisions I make then. And if I don't know exactly what I would do in a certain circumstance, I pray about it, and there always seems to be an answer that always comes. I still write in a journal, things that really impact me, or Scripture that I've read, or something I've read in my devotions.

I write it in this journal, and I go back often and re-read those comments or the pieces of knowledge that are there. I love to sing, even though I don't sing well, I love to sing. I have a CD or my radio on the way, driving, all the time, and I sing along and praise Him through that. I'm learning to lift my hands in praise, and not being afraid to do that. I like to send notes of gratitude to people who maybe need some encouragement, because I believe that's part of His ministry for me, too, is to be thankful and to share that with others through a note of encouragement.

I try to be very, very aware of when I need to be thankful and then let someone know that they have touched my life. I think probably being open and transparent as much as I can, has helped me through it all and again, I still grieve, but I know I need to go on, that God wants me to pick up the pieces and go on.

Sue Farmer is wise and her husband was one of our wise elders.

ACTION STEPS FOR OUR STORY

At Connection Pointe Christian Church, I've learned that wise leaders craft wise plans and cast a wise vision.

1. Craft a vision for your church.

    What is the vision for your church? If you're a preacher you may say, "I'm not sure. I'm just trying to put together a good sermon for this Sunday." If you're an elder, you may say, "As long as the people are getting along and our bills are paid, we're happy."

    If I were to ask one of your members, as they entered your church building on Sunday, "What is the vision for your church?" what would they say?

    Every church needs to regularly ask, "What's our business?" and "How's business?" That is why you must craft a vision that supports the values of your church, then cast it to the congregation and make plans to carry it out.

    The reason you need to establish your vision is because it focuses the energy of the people on what you're trying to do. Federal Express has a stated mission for their company which says, "We are determined to get every letter and package delivered by 10:30 the next day." As a result of that stated mission, the energy of the employees is focused on accomplishing it.

    In a similar way, the church must surely know what the vision is and how we hope to get there. Connection Pointe Christian Church has grown from a church of 200 to over 4,000 in the last thirty-one years. That *never* would have happened if the leadership had not developed a vision and a strategic plan.

2. Define a vision that reflects the priorities and values of the congregation.

What is vision

Vision is a specific plan to accomplish tangible objectives, which should be reviewed and measured regularly.

3. Form a collaborative team who will craft the vision.

How do you get others involved in the vision

Begin with the leaders to develop the vision.

It's important to note that the preacher does *not* have to be *the* visionary. Some preachers are more gifted as teachers, shepherds, or evangelists than as visionary leaders. That's OK. In that case, he can build a team who can make the vision happen. As long as you understand the *value* of a *clear* vision, even if you aren't the visionary, vision can still be crafted if you will ask for help.

In our situation, I went on a retreat with our elders, shortly after I came, and we crafted a vision together. We developed a mission statement, discussed values that supported it and some plans to carry it out. We reviewed our strategic plan every year. The last major initiative we accomplished was called "Unstoppable." (You can read about it in chapter 4.)

How is the vision crafted

- Brainstorm with no evaluation or comments allowed. (All elders and staff)
- Every elder and staff member is given a chance to rate the items.
- A ranking is finalized.
- A narrative is written.
- A strategic plan is developed. (How we're going to get there.)
- Expand the group and seek the input of others concerning their perceptions of the initial vision.

4. Set a time to communicate the vision with the congregation.

Make sure your vision is clear and openly communicate it to the entire congregation

Don't be afraid to ask for feedback and be prepared for resistance or, at least, hesitancy. But remember: WHAT YOU RESIST, PERSISTS.

Thirty years ago, as we changed our worship style, there was feedback. Lots of it! I remember saying to some members who were "concerned" about the direction of the church, "The elders will be glad to visit with you and others ... this Saturday morning from 9-11 AM."

They came ... all three of them ... and we listened. They were still an active part of our church until they went to Heaven, even though we did not change the vision of the church. (They just needed to know that we really *heard* their concerns.) It is important to understand that *listening* to the feedback of members concerning the direction of your ministry does not mean that you'll change what you're doing.

Another way to seek their input is through the use of surveys, which we have done a number of times.

Strategic planning is not just announcing the destination, it's about managing the journey

You *regularly* say, "Here's our plan ... what do you think?"

JESUS' FIFTH PRIORITY: LEADERSHIP

Jesus is often granted the distinction of being the most significant and successful leader of all time. His relevance has extended more than 2,000 years and His ministry, death, and resurrection spawned Christianity, the largest faith community in the world.

His influence in contemporary society, even in what may be reasonably called a post-Christian American culture, far exceeds any other philosopher, poet, or religious figure. Unlike any other, Jesus' wisdom was perfect.

However, His leadership priority has implications for us today as He continues to influence generations of people called to tend His sheep, love His bride, and lead the body over which Christ is the head. Jesus modeled leadership grounded in humility and marked by a servant's heart. He showed in very personal and practical ways that we are called to look beyond our own selves, our own needs, and our own desires to recognize that the gift that we have been given has nothing to do with our worthiness so it is impossible to reasonably adopt an attitude of arrogance, pride, or self-achievement.

We serve others because it is the natural outflow of the way Jesus has served us by giving His life as a ransom. This priority also emerges from the way Jesus pursued his earthly ministry. He knew that He had to die to achieve God's vision of redemption and Jesus carefully managed and protected that vision. He understood that a God-sized vision required diligent self-leadership and also leadership of others.

He looked ahead to the eventual formation of His Church and prepared leaders who could effectively model servant leadership in His absence, to a time when His disciples would lead the Church and establish roles and functions that align with Jesus' example and effectively support the work of each local congregation.

CHAPTER SIX

RESTORED FAMILIES

If Restored People lead to Restored Churches, the same can be said of Restored Families. Psalm 127:1 reads, "Unless the LORD builds a house, the work of the builders is wasted" (NLT).

That is true, regarding the Lord's house *and* our individual houses.

Before I went to seminary, I remember a long discussion with my mother, about preachers and their families. Even though I had been given a good role model, in Max Hickerson's family (my pastor growing up), I was very aware of the predominant opinion that many people have of the preacher's family: "They aren't really committed, their marriages aren't really healthy, and their children often rebel."

While those observations are often true, that is no excuse for preachers to neglect their families for the sake of "church work."

So, I went to seminary and into full-time ministry determined to prioritize my wife and kids. My intentions were good, but the "adrenaline rush" of full-time ministry, still took precedence over my family, honestly, for too many weeks of those forty years of pastoral ministry.

In fact, it started in 1980, the year I became the lead pastor of a church of 450 people, when I was only twenty-five years old. After dinner, one night in 1980, I gave my wife a kiss on the cheek as I headed out for another night of "ministry." As I was leaving I glanced back at her and she was clearly fighting back tears.

I came over to her and asked if something was wrong. She was hesitant to level with me, but after my persistence, she finally just asked me a few questions: "Where were you last night? The night before? The night before that?"

My answer was simple: I had been discipling couples four nights a week, as we made appointments with prospective members and visited in their homes. I trained and took with me, a different couple every Monday through Thursday night. It was thrilling to see people make commitments to Christ and the Church, *and* a joy to see each couple become effective witnesses for Jesus and the Church.

My wife knew that to be true, so she had been hesitant to confront me about never being home at night during the week. After all, how dare she become an obstacle to my calling to "seek and save the lost."

So, she reasoned ... But God had to get my attention early on that preachers *can* allow "ministry" to wound their families in the process. It's interesting that one of the characteristics of a preaching elder, mentioned in 1 Timothy 3:4-5, "He must manage his own family well, having children who respect and obey him. For if a man cannot manage his own household, how can he take care of God's church?" (NLT)

Back to my crucial conversation with my wife that night. When I admitted that I'd been out "saving the world," a distance was developing between Kristen and me. We took out the calendar and I had not taken a 24-hour day off in the first six months of my ministry!

I wish I could say that I never again put her and the kids *after* the priority of ministry. But I *cannot* say that. Years later, we had another crucial conversation about my presence at home.

I had taken Fridays off, after that initial confrontation, and continued to do so for the next twenty-seven years. However, often I was home but not *really* home. She said, "You're here, but you are always reading or doing church work."

Gratefully, I heeded her counsel and did better over time, but the "temptation" to neglect the family for the work of the ministry was always a battle.

So, before we discuss "Restored Families," I need to say "thank you" to my wife for her patience with me and commitment to me, as I was a slow learner when it came to the family as my Number One priority, after *my* personal connection with Christ.

I didn't miss many of the kids' games or concerts, we have had a "weekly date" most weeks, and I had one-on-one time with the kids regularly as well. We also made the commitment to get out of the area code at least once a quarter.

But now, as I adjust to my recent "retirement," I am grateful to say that my wife and I have been married for forty-one years, and all of our kids love the Lord and spend lots of time with us, now that we have an "empty nest."

For that I am extremely thankful, but I really know that most of the credit goes to my wife, my kids, and my gracious God.

So, I am still an ongoing work of Restoration when it comes to nurturing a Restored Family.

RESTORING ME

God created the world ... He planted a garden called Eden. He formed Adam from the dust of the earth and placed him in the Garden.

Then He created the first parade. All the animals paraded past Adam and he was given the privilege of naming them. Each animal had a mate, but none of the animals were as special as this man, made in the image of God.

God sedated Adam before surgery, and then took out a rib and stitched him back up. From that rib, God created a mate for Adam. She was not like the animals, which he would dominate. She would be a partner. Mothers have a bond with their sons and daughters, but the union between the husband and the wife should be the primary relationship in the home.

Adam said in Genesis 2:23, ... "This one is bone from my bone, and flesh from my flesh! She will be called 'woman,' because she was taken from 'man'" (NLT.) "Wow! This creature is like me. I will call her, literally in the Hebrew: 'Taken out of me' -- 'wo-man!'"

A boy was playing with friends, as they ran down a hill. That Sunday's lesson had been on God creating Eve from Adam's side. As they were running, a boy screamed, "Wait up, guys. I think I'm having a wife!"

Back to our story ... Eve was deceived by Satan into disobeying God, and her partner, Adam, chose to disobey God, as well.

(Adam valued his relationship with Eve more than his relationship to God.)

Since that was the root of Adam's sin, that would be part of the consequences. Eve would now have pain in childbirth. Her home would be under attack, even during the celebration of a birth.

Her passion would still be for her husband, but his response would be selfish. She would give him honor and respect, but he would use that authority for his own comfort and control. The partnership would be under attack. There would be unequal giving in the marriage partnership.

The husband would try to treat his wife the way he treated the animals, as possessions. So sin not only fractured our relationship with God, but our relationships with each other. We hear of domestic violence, in the news, almost every week. (Men physically mistreating their wives or live-in girlfriends.)

Ogden Nash was known for his short witty poems: More than forty years ago, my Pastor gave me a sermon he'd preached on marriage, and it began with Ogden Nash's poem: "To keep your marriage brimming with love in the loving cup, whenever you're wrong, admit it. Whenever you're right, shut up!"

The *Good* News is that Jesus came to restore our souls *and* our families, under His control, back to God.

Ephesians 5:21 is the best instruction ever given on marriage: "Submit to one another out of reverence for Christ" (NLT).

Restored couples understand …

We mutually submit

The Scripture does *not* say, "Submit to each other unless you are married." For marriage to be a partnership, *each* partner, must submit: Mutual Submission! So …

The wife submits

Ephesians 5:22-24, "For wives, this means submit to your husbands as to the Lord. For a husband is the head of his wife as Christ is the head of the church. He is the Savior of his body, the church. As the church submits to Christ, so you wives should submit to your husbands in everything" (NLT).

Just as Christ works through the church, to accomplish His purpose in the world, and in the community, the wife is to submit to her husband in this partnership.

I heard there were two lines in Heaven, one for dominant husbands and one for submissive husbands. The submissive husband line extended almost out of sight. And there was only one man in the dominant husband line.

He was small, timid, and did not seem very dominant. When the angel asked why he was in that line, he just said, "My wife told me to stand here!"

Anyway, because men are weak and selfish, it is difficult to trust us with leadership in the home. Too many times, men have used authority and respect to take *advantage* of those "under" their care.

Wives, you can really put the heat on us husbands by … praying for us and trusting *God* to work on us. In other words, any authority comes from God.

Romans 13:1 reads, "…For all authority comes from God, and those in positions of authority have been placed there by God" (NLT).

First Peter 3:1-2 says, "You wives must accept the authority of your husbands. Then, even if some refuse to obey the Good News, your godly lives will speak to them without any words. They will be won over by observing your pure and reverent lives" (NLT).

God uses authority to deal with the ungodly attitudes in us and He rewards godly attitudes.

Now, you might be thinking, "But you don't know my husband. He'll take advantage of that authority, if I give it to him." (Obviously, if there is physical, sexual, mental or verbal abuse in the home, you need to seek godly counsel … And do what you need to do to protect you or your children from danger.)

But apart from that, even though I don't know your husband, I *do* know your God!

Proverbs 21:1 says, "The king's heart is like a stream of water directed by the LORD; he guides it wherever he pleases" (NLT). God is faithful! He will move your husband to make decisions for reasons only *he* understands, but God can reach him through something the husband understands.

It *could* be that you have not seen God work in your husband's life because He is still working on your attitude or lack of trust in the home.

(Women, before you close this book, please keep reading …)

The husband also submits

Ephesians 5:25-26, "For husbands, this means love your wives, just as Christ loved the church. He gave up his life for her to make her holy and clean, washed by the cleansing of God's word" (NLT).

Wives, did you notice that you are to trust the Lord by respecting your husband … But the husband is to love his wife, "…just as Christ loved the church … He gave His life for her."

How much did Christ love His bride, the church? He was killed so that she (we) could be restored and live forever with Him in Heaven.

Men, we are to give ourselves up for our wives, as Christ did for us: to make us complete and clean.

Ephesians 5:28, "In the same way, husbands ought to love their wives as they love their own bodies. For a man who loves his wife actually shows love for himself" (NLT).

Let's keep it real: I love my wife deeply, but she does a better job in her role of submission and respect than I do, demonstrating Christ's love toward her!

Jesus sacrificed *everything* to honor His bride. He submitted to her needs, her pleasure, her glory.

But, men, our battle with the sinful nature is that we often live in relationship with her, so we can benefit. Right?

If you are married, would you sit down with your wife or husband, and repeat these words to each other:

HUSBANDS: "I ask for your respect and submission … and I promise to love and respect you, as Christ loved the church."

WIVES: "I ask for your respect and submission … and I promise to love and respect you, as the church submits to Christ."

Husbands, you may now kiss your wives!

RESTORING THE CHURCH

We all should *mutually* submit, wives should submit, husbands should submit … And …

The church submits

Ephesians 5:30-33, "We are members of his body. As the Scriptures say, "A man leaves his father and mother and is joined to his wife, and the two are united into one." This is a great mystery, but it is an illustration of the way Christ and the church are one. So again I say, each man must love his wife as he loves himself, and the wife must respect her husband" (NLT).

As Paul writes, he is in awe of what the Holy Spirit has said, "This is a great mystery …" This is amazing … this is supernatural.

Remember Paul is not married! In fact, if you are single, that is *not* a consolation prize!

Paul said in 1 Corinthians 7:7, "I wish everyone were single, just as I am. Yet each person has a special gift from God, of one kind or another" (NLT).

He had the gift of singleness. He was content as a single adult. So, when he says, "Marriage is an illustration of how Christ and the church are one…" He is amazed! It's a great mystery!

But I believe, these last few verses are written to *every person* in the church; those married and those who are single.

Because … marriage is just a picture of the kind of relationship we, in the church, have with Christ.

We are all children of God, through faith in Jesus' sacrifice for our sins. And, since the church is called "the Bride of Christ," we should love the local church, the way Christ has loved us!

One of the primary blessings of full-time ministry is to see families become Restored to God. In fact, my wife and I have had two full-time ministries. Nine years in Cincy and thirty-one years at Connection Pointe Christian Church in Indy.

One family has been a part of *both* churches. I asked our friend, Kathy, to write about their family's Restoration to God through these two churches. Recently, she wrote me this letter:

"We were married on Saturday, July 7, 1979. You did our wedding because the senior pastor was going to be out of town that weekend.

A little over a year later, toward the end of September, you came to Cincinnati Children's Hospital Medical Center to visit a church member's niece. I was working that day in the Rehab area and had her as my patient. I talked with you and reminded you that you had done our wedding the summer before. We had a nice chat. I thought to myself, 'We should try to start going to church there.'

Less than a week later, on September 26, 1980 my dad died suddenly at home of a heart attack. We had moved there back in 1971 and had never had a church home. We did not know who to call and you were really the only pastor I had ever had contact with (other than the pastor at Mike's Baptist church). I was hoping you would remember seeing me at the hospital and I called you that day my father died to see if you could perform the funeral. You remembered seeing me at the hospital and you and Kristen came right over to the house and talked with me, my sister, and my mom.

Shortly after the funeral our first son was born on October 9. We were busy with the baby, I worked every other weekend at the hospital and we still never got around going to church. Julie was born on October 15, 1882. Not quite two years later in the late winter/early spring of 1984 we talked and decided we should start making a point to go to church. We wanted the kids to be in Sunday School. Mike had a friend who went there and I had become friends with his wife. We began attending church there and went about every weekend.

I was pregnant with Daniel. On June 3, 1984 Daniel was born a few weeks early with many congenital problems. The doctors told us his condition was basically incompatible with life. He lived fifteen days and passed away on October 18, 1984. During those weeks, you made a couple of visits to sit with me at the hospital and see Daniel. When he died, you performed the small family service we had.

Your youngest son, Nate, came home from the hospital that

day. He was born on the day Daniel passed away. Afterward you came to the house to check on us a few days later. I mentioned that I was worried that I had never been baptized, only christened as a baby, and you called a church member to come watch the two kids and we went up to the church and I was baptized that very day.

We began attending church regularly after that. During the time immediately after Danny died, the church was so supportive, sending food and cards from people we didn't even know. I began working in the church nursery and I remember taking care of Nate, your son. When he would cry the other women would always hand him to me. They would say I have the same hair as Kristen and maybe he'll think you are her! We so enjoyed our church family and listening to you preach every week. During that time, my mom and my sister were baptized, as were some of our best friends.

You left a couple of years later in 1986. I had a miscarriage on June 3, 1986 -- Danny's birthday. We decided then, we wouldn't have any more kids. At the end of that year we were building a new house and had sold ours. A church member had been our realtor. We had to move in with my mom. The day the builder dug the foundation for our basement Mike found out we were moving to Indy. I called you and said, 'How far is Brownsburg from Indianapolis?'

We talked on the phone and we eventually came for the weekend. Our builder was willing to transfer our house to a subdivision they were building an hour north of the church where you now were ... We went up there to look at it and it was very nice. However, the drive was too much for us to attend church and church activities every week, so we opted to move to Brownsburg. Mike had to come early and was living in a hotel and we had to wait until we could get our loan approved.

We finally moved in the last weekend of April,1987. My birthday was May 1 and I remember our oldest son being so worried that we were in a new place and I wouldn't know anyone to celebrate my birthday with. He said, 'Maybe the Reeves can come for your birthday!'

Anyway, the rest is history. The following year on July 8, 1988 (a day after our anniversary!) another son was born. God had a plan that we didn't know about! We were so grateful he was healthy! We have been church members since then and our family has been so blessed having Brownsburg Christian Church/Connection Pointe Christian Church as our church home."

Then she added:

"One more thing: When we began coming to BCC, everyone was so friendly and made us feel at home. We joined your Sunday School Class. Many of the members were a little older than us but they took us under their wing. It was so easy to become a part of this church because everyone made us feel at home. The following summer, our son was born, and now he is married, preparing to become a physician, and he and his wife serve in the children's ministry and are 'All In' at Connection Pointe Christian Church."

Kathy would later learn that they were my *first* wedding … She joked that if she'd known that, they'd have contacted another pastor. She thinks that's funny … and I do too!

When they learned that his new job was forty minutes from our church, they said, "We don't care how far away it is from work, we want to live where you are pastor."

So … for thirty-eight of my forty years in pastoral ministry, they have been part of the congregation. I have joked with them, "If there was such a thing as purgatory, you are 'paid up.'"

I have now performed weddings for their three children, offered prayers over each child and grandchild on "Parental Commitment" Days … And all three adult children, as well as Mike and Kathy, are still "All In" members of Connection Pointe (our new church name since 2004).

When families and churches have been *Restored*, there is *nothing* like being deeply connected to Christ, the Head of the Church, and experiencing the blessings that come when we see Restored Families. Our two families have now been restored together for nearly four decades!

We should also respect the church and trust God to guide, protect and care for His church through His delegated leaders in the church.

In other words, we may not always understand all that is going on, but we can always trust the Head of the church, Jesus Christ. He knows exactly what He is doing, behind the scenes.

So we commit ourselves to Him and His church like families should commit to each other.

And then, when the whole family is "All In" … It is fun to watch!

In our relationships, in our families, and in the church, let's become Restored back to *His* plan for mutual submission … honoring each other above ourselves … and following the Head of the church, Jesus Christ! (through the delegated authority of the elders) … and ultimately submitting to Jesus because … He *should* be the Head of *every* family and home … And He *is* the only Head of the Church!

In September 2016, when my wife and I announced our plan to retire from the lead pastor role at Connection Pointe Christian Church, we thanked this wonderful congregation for the more than thirty years of love, encouragement, and growth we have experienced with and through them.

I then told them, "The greatest blessing we've received from God, through this congregation, is a love for His Church." All three of our children, and our daughters-in-law, are active in the Lord's work. They love each other, they love Connection Pointe Christian Church, and they love Mom and Dad (Gigi and Papa to the grandkids)!

They are all in their thirties. Many of their generation are saying, "You lost me," to the Church, in general. *Why do our kids love the Lord and His Church?* Because they have watched a church, for over three decades, being Restored and granting our family much kindness and love.

In thirty years, the only time I was "confronted" by our chairman of the elders was to ask me direct, invasive, personal questions like, "Are you spending personal time with each of your three children? Are you caring for the *most important family* in this church, *your* immediate family, the way you shepherd our church family?"

You may ask, "What age were your children when the elders asked you those questions?" At every stage for thirty-one years, that has always been their #1 question: "Are you giving priority time to your family?"

In fact, they "forced" my wife and me to have alone time.

Elders of all churches … Are you listening? For our fifth anniversary, they sent us to Cancun! For year ten? … Hawaii! Year fifteen? … Grand Cayman Islands … Our twentieth anniversary with the church? … Hawaii! For our twenty-fifth? … Italy! When year thirty approached, my "more spiritual than me" wife said, "You have done so much for us, don't pay for us to go on another beautiful vacation." (I wouldn't have said that to them, but she did.)

Instead, they established a Legacy Fund in our name, funded by church members above their weekly tithes to the "storehouse." We can use those funds to help under-resourced churches, church leaders and/or young adults who are preparing for full-time ministry.

You tell me why our kids love the Lord and His Church! Healthy, Restored Churches produce healthy, restored families!

ACTION STEPS FOR OUR STORY

Our elders wisely discerned that while it *is* essential for the church to be Restored to Spiritual Health, it is just as important that the preacher be aware of these *Obstacles to Restoring Me.*

1. Discuss potential obstacles to becoming a Restored Church Family.
    A healthy church must be led by healthy leaders.
    Leaders: Are you accumulating believers or developing disciples? Are you attracting crowds or allowing God to shape a congregation?

2. How can we ensure that our homes and churches are well-fed?
    Healthy churches and families must be led to Restoration by Christ, not just be inspired by skillful leaders or our own *personal* "wisdom."
    Just as we must feed our families the Word of God at home, we must feed our congregations the Word of God when we meet.
    Leaders: Are you bringing the people of God to the mountain of God?

3. As church leaders, determine to be as devoted to your family as to the Church Family.
    Healthy leaders do not just "succeed" with Jesus' bride, the Church,

but they also nurture their bride, at home.

Ultimately, church leader, you will treat *Jesus'* bride the same way you treat *your* bride.

4.   Never lose sight of the primary mission of the church.

Healthy leaders will use God's search light to reach the lost and search our own souls.

I heard a wise leader suggest that church leaders should set apart three days a week just to be open to God's work in my soul and His conviction of my inner struggles.

JESUS' SIXTH PRIORITY: THE HURTING

Most people are living with some kind of resource deficit, whether that be a lack of money, energy, or time. Some suffer from a physical or mental challenge that stands as an obstacle to self-sufficiency, peace, freedom, or hope. Others are living with some type of relational dysfunction, often revolving around a romance, co-worker, or family. We rub shoulders with these people every day and it is tempting to associate these problems with the degradation of contemporary society, with laziness, or just bad luck.

As Jesus demonstrated so clearly and consistently, however, all of these conclusions represent faulty thinking. The fact of the matter is that the way believers view and engage people in need should be totally unrelated to the factors that created the need. Instead, followers of Christ should see every person first and foremost as being made in the image of God, being endowed with inherent value that exceeds any other animal, plant, or even the most rare metal and jewel.

On this backdrop it is much easier to understand Jesus' interaction with the crowds. He addressed physical needs to create margin for and/or to prompt consideration of the underlying spiritual condition and He felt a deep sense of compassion for people who were suffering emotionally, physically, and spiritually.

And His perspectives serve as an example to the Church as believers strive to seek out the hurting in the world around us and to view them through Christ's eyes, to eliminate the arrogance that so easily produces cynicism, fear, and pessimism that stand as a barrier to a compassionate and loving response.

And as Jesus leveraged physical healing to encourage spiritual transformation, the Church too must provide relevant ministries that restore marriages and estranged family relationships, that overcome strongholds, and that meet physical needs as a strategy to open doors for people to experience a personal and reconciled relationship with God through Christ.

Jesus said in Revelation 3:20, "If you hear my voice and open the door, I will come in, and we will share a meal together as friends" (NLT).

He makes time to eat with us and we must make time to eat with our families.

CHAPTER SEVEN

RESTORED RESPECT

My wife and I have been enriched through the two church families we've led and by our three children. They are now in their thirties. Our sons are married to fine Christian women. Our daughter has many Christian friends. All three of them love the Lord, are active in evangelical churches, and are now some of the best and wisest "peers" my wife and I enjoy.

None of the five of us are perfect, by a long shot, but we *are* grateful that none of the three ever walked away from the Lord's restoration of their souls.

Our older two were more strong-willed, like their (ahem) mother. (Anyone who knows her and me, understands that I am the "risk taker" and stronger-willed.) However, our youngest son is more like his mother.

Now that he is the dad of a toddler, we recently enjoyed reading a "rebellious" note from our youngest, when he was fifteen. He had just "messed up," by not being home on time. It is the closest he ever came to being "disrespectful."

Dear parents,

Thanks for always being there for me. For all the times you've watched me play football to helping me on my homework. But most of all thanks for bringing me into this world. I'm so thankful for having loving Christian parents. Without you I would probably not be the same kid I am today. Now I understand why you do the things you do it's to help me stay out of trouble. And to help me with my future as an adult. Although sometimes I don't realize it, but you are the most loving, caring, people in the world. For all the times you've changed you're schedules to do something with me. Something so little like just to help me on something or just to talk. Another great thing about you is that you encourage me to do my best in school and in sports. Not just me but Danielle and Jared too. It's pretty sad that I don't think you are the best people in the world sometimes. That just makes me mad at myself for not realizing how bad I allow myself to get. Thank you for being the most loving, caring, most forgiving people in the world (sorry but God's the most in heaven.)

Love,
Nate
9-8-98

RESTORING ME

Children are a blessing … usually. Some expectant fathers were in a waiting room, their wives were in the process of delivering. A nurse came and told one man his wife had given birth to twins. "Whoa! I play for the Minnesota Twins." A little later, the nurse came and said, "you have triplets." "What? I work for the 3M Company." The third guy slipped off his chair and laid on the floor!

"Are you ok?" "No…I work for the 7-Up Company!"

In the Old Testament, the *sin* nature was in the child. The Jewish children were to know the Scriptures, they were taught to pray for God's help to obey, and that act of faith gave them grace.

But the sin nature has always been with us. In the New Testament, Jesus came and grace was fully revealed.

Unfortunately, society has swung from raising and disciplining children to tolerating and spoiling them.

But children and parents still need discipline. The tendency is to have a home full of love, but not enough discipline, or have a home with discipline, but not enough compassion.

The first three verses of Ephesians 6 are spoken to children. One of the ways this church began to grow, in the late eighties, was the result of an outreach to children and their families. Every June, the numbers were larger than the year before.

Vacation Bible School. We always had VBS, the first week after school was out. Always during the morning, Monday through Friday. My mother was the Director of Vacation Bible School at Standard Publishing Co. in Cincinnati. The VBS materials they produced were their #1 product.

My mom always felt that VBS should be during the week, in the morning. Many churches started having VBS at night – "Easier to get workers." But I always insisted we had VBS in the morning the first week after school. You say, "What's wrong with evening VBS?" (Nothing!) But morning VBS was an outreach for "unchurched" children and their families.

We always had a VBS Carnival on Friday. I was given the same job every year … "Dunk the Pastor." When our daughter was in the second grade, she stepped up to throw the ball and hit the target, in which case, the chair I was sitting on, would give way and I'd get dunked!

On her last throw, she missed, but the staff cheated and let her run up and push the target … I had spread out on the seat, so my foot was outside the tank.

Well … when she pushed the lever, I dropped into the water, but not before my heel hit the metal rim around the tank. So … we went to get stitches. A nurse from church walked in and said, "Will you *ever* grow up?" I responded, "I sure hope not!"

We're all kids at heart, aren't we?

Jesus loved children so much that He gave this warning: Matthew 18:6, "If you cause one of these little ones who trusts in me to fall into sin, it would be better for you to have a large millstone tied around your neck and be drowned in the depths of the sea" (NLT).

None of us had perfect parents and none of us are perfect parents. Because every parent is a sinner like every other human being. Parents need to learn and grow just like children do. No matter what your home is like, God loves you.

When you're struggling, He cares and wants to help you. When things are going well, He's also there, hoping you won't forget Him, but will be thankful for His blessings.

Usually, the way children think about their parents is how they will think about God. God is in charge, He is the authority, but, He has delegated the authority, parents, in your home to you. (When children learn to obey their parents, they learn to obey God.)

God does love us the way we are, but He also loves us too much to let us stay that way. Let's see God's plan to "Restore Respect."

We must revere God

Two reasons: Ephesians 6:1, "Children, obey your parents because you belong to the Lord, for this is the right thing to do" (NLT).

In the Jewish culture, a child could only be removed from God's delegated authority of the parents, if the child married ("leave and cleave"). Or ... When the child became thirty. Jesus began His ministry at thirty, because He had obeyed His parents, but then had to be released at thirty, to speak directly from God's authority.

We are to revere / respect / obey God because we belong to Him ... it's the right thing to do!

Disobedience is a very serious sin, which leads to other sins.

Romans 1:28-30, "Since they thought it foolish to acknowledge God ... Their lives became full of every kind of wickedness, sin, greed, hate, envy, murder, quarreling, deception, malicious behavior, and gossip. They are backstabbers, haters of God, insolent, proud, and boastful. They invent new ways of sinning, and they disobey their parents" (NLT).

It all begins with obeying God and then your parents. Parents, if you have to say something twice, they did *not* obey. Delayed obedience is disobedience ... or ... the "countdown." If you have to count down for them to obey, they are not respecting you ... They are playing a game *with* you.

Obedience is not obedience unless it is immediate. When Jesus was a child, He was obedient to His parents. If Jesus was ever disobedient, that would have been a sin. And Scripture says He never sinned. So, He never disobeyed His parents. (Even though they were not without sin.)

I heard about the parents of a four-year-old driving home after church and as they pulled out of the church parking lot, they noticed their son was whimpering in the back seat. They asked him what was wrong. Through tears, he said, "The pastor said he wanted us to be raised in a Christian home, but I want to stay with you guys!"

Raising kids to love the Lord is a difficult assignment. But, Mom and Dad, God wants you to revere Him and then model the way God expects obedience.

Sometimes parents say, "We take our kids to church so they will learn to love God." But it is not the Church's job or a Christian school teacher's job. The *primary* responsibility of teaching a healthy reverence for God is *your* responsibility, Mom and Dad.

Now, of course, you need secondary influences like children/student ministries and Christian teachers/coaches to help you, but it starts with you!

You have the strongest emotional investment in your child. So, jump in and enjoy the privilege of parenting.

Babysitters, relatives, daycare workers, and church leaders never will give an account to God for how they raised *your* children. *You will!*

We must honor others

Ephesians 6:2-3, "'Honor your father and mother.' This is the first commandment with a promise: If you honor your father and mother, 'things will go well for you, and you will have a long life on the earth'" (NLT).

Obedience is doing what the parents say. Honoring is accepting the *values* behind the commands. In the early years, teach them to obey. In the later years, teach them values to guide their lives.

When a child is told to take out the trash and they do it, while complaining and sneering, they might be obedient but they are not honoring. God says parents should be obeyed and honored.

If a child disrespects his parents, he is disrespecting the God who provided the parents. If kids are allowed to talk back to their parents or say bad things about them, or roll their eyes at them, the kids are *not* honoring their parents.

However, when we become adults, we don't have to obey our parents, but we still must *honor* them!

When we sin, there are consequences ... and there *should* be consequences when children do not obey or honor their parents ... Never discipline or punish a child when you are angry. It will wound deeply and leave a scar on the heart. Discipline should be carried out, in love, by a parent who is under control. As you discipline your children for not obeying or dishonoring, there are different ways to teach them, depending on their age. A six-year-old may not get play time. A nine-year-old may not be permitted to watch TV. A thirteen-year-old could lose their cell phone for the week.

If they're in high school, maybe no cell phone and no car keys. In college, if they choose to major in partying, you stop paying tuition. "Honor the Lord and us, or do not expect us to fund your 'season of experimentation.'"

Parents, do you have a strong-willed child? I've had them and I *was* one ... still am! But strong-willed children will test your boundaries. They'll try to move the line. You stay strong, Mom and Dad ... Don't negotiate with your child.

Proverbs 19:18, "Discipline your children while there is hope. Otherwise you will ruin their lives" (NLT).

Proverbs 29:17, "Discipline your children, and they will give you peace of mind and will make your heart glad" (NLT).

Consistently teach them how to obey and honor ... If you don't, who will?

We must discipline ourselves

Question: What is "provoking your children to anger?"

Ephesians 6:4, "Fathers, do not provoke your children to anger by the way you treat them" (NLT).

Colossians 3:21, "Fathers, do not aggravate your children, or they will become discouraged" (NLT).

The way you treat them, you can discourage them.

Proverbs 22:6, "Direct your children onto the right path, and when they are older, they will not leave it" (NLT).

To "direct" them is more than just going to church. It means to teach them patience, how to stay strong under pressure, and how to be reasonable in an unreasonable world.

When we discipline with anger, impatience, frustration, and cruelty, our kids will likely handle life the way you disciplined *them* (out of control).

It is a privilege to be a parent. The greatest blessing to come into your home is a child. And how 'bout grandchildren? Don't you think grandparents should have them first? Just sayin'!

But, with privilege comes responsibility. The Bible says Enoch walked with God *after* Methuselah was born. (Do ya think there's a connection?)

Genesis 5:22, "After the birth of Methuselah, Enoch lived in close fellowship with God for another 300 years, and he had other sons and daughters" (NLT).

Many kids leave church from age eighteen to twenty-two, but many come back after the birth of *their* first child. (Parents have everything to do with bringing their child into the world, and they will have a lot to do with where they go, when they leave this world.)

If you raise them to know the Lord early on, they have a significantly greater chance of being connected to the Lord, throughout life and forever!

The problem often is that the *parents* will not *discipline themselves* to remain consistent for the child.

First Kings 1:6 says of Adonijah, "His father, King David, had never disciplined him at any time, even by asking, 'Why are you doing that?'" (NLT) Later Adonijah decided to take his father's throne and it did not go well, He died a tragic, early death. His brother Absalom was also spoiled and suffered in a similar way.

Eli the priest was undisciplined as a father, and God said about Eli in 1 Samuel 3:13, "I have warned him that judgment is coming upon his family forever, because his sons are blaspheming God and he hasn't disciplined them" (NLT).

Your son and/or daughter has a free will. Even if you teach them to obey, honor, and you discipline yourself, they *still* could rebel. (That's the point behind Jesus' parable, in Luke 15, of the Prodigal Son.)

So ... you pray, hope, trust and wait for them to return to the Lord and you. But there is no guarantee that they will. You cannot make them do right. But according to Ephesians 6:4, we are to, "...bring them up with the discipline and instruction that comes from the Lord" (NLT).

The word for "bring them up" is a tender word, like the warm nest of a mother bird. Every child needs our unconditional love ... no matter how they look, act, are gifted or not gifted.

So ... how do kids know of your unconditional love? Love is spelled T-I-M-E. Not M-O-N-E-Y or T-H-I-N-G-S!

I don't remember the "things" I received as a kid as much as I remember the time spent, praying for and encouraging me. I can still hear my mom's voice, at every game and every sport. "Come on, Steve!" (Every time I went to bat in baseball)

Birthdays, upside-down pineapple cake, just for me. Whether it was my first sermon ... or the last one, before she went to Heaven, when it was just her and me, at her home, she'd say, "Read this week's sermon to me." Then she'd say, "I can't imagine anyone *not* accepting Jesus after hearing that message!" (Moms are so objective, aren't they?)

Parents, our kids don't want stuff, they want you! (It takes more discipline to give them you, than it does to give them things.)

Dad, Mom, you have a choice to make: Your TV, your hobbies, or your kids? There's not enough of you for everything; something has to go (especially in the season when they're growing up).

I heard about two kids whose dad was always working ... absent from the dinner table. They fought over who got to sit in dad's chair. The son beat his sister to dad's chair and said, "I'm not just going to sit here, I'll be dad tonight."

His sister said, "you're not dad; if you're so smart, what is seven times seventy-seven?" Without even looking up, the boy said, "Go ask your mother!"

Mom and Dad, discipline yourself ... give them time, encouragement, and consistent love. For every word of criticism, give seven statements of encouragement!

Let me say it another way ... The closer you are to your children, the more *likely* they are to accept your discipline!

We've all rebelled. So, there's a time to discipline, a time to repent, and a time to forgive. But you have to establish the *routine* ... the rules and the expectations.

So ... be consistent, and discipline yourself, and it will reduce the mixed messages, confusion, and drama in your home.

RESTORING THE CHURCH

We must mentor learners

This is the most difficult part for many parents. To mentor them means: *Raise* them, so you can *release* them.

Now, I've noticed if you have more than one child, it becomes easier to release them, with each child.

Child #1 – Three months before you take them to the church nursery.

Child #2 – Six weeks (half the time it took with Child #1).

Child #3 – You call the church from the hospital, to register that child for the nursery! (Can we leave him there from 8:00-12:30?)

Hannah, in the Old Testament, knew she'd have to release Samuel, after God miraculously gave her Samuel.

In 1 Samuel 1:27-28a, Hannah told Eli the priest, "I asked the LORD to give me this boy, and he has granted my request. Now I am giving him to the LORD…" (NLT).

Give them roots so they can grow, and wings, so they can fly!

We must empower leaders

First Samuel 1:28, "…and he will belong to the Lord his whole life" (NLT).

Hannah asked God for a child. God gave her a son. Then she gave him back to God for ministry.

Wise mothers know it's nice to be needed, but the *ultimate* goal is to empower them to follow the Lord, independent of her.

Ephesians 6:4 again, "…bring them up with the discipline and instruction that comes from the Lord" (NLT).

The only way we can teach our kids to love Jesus is to love Him ourselves.

ACTION STEPS FOR OUR STORY

1. What does a faithful church leader look like?

    Respected church leaders *are* faithful.

    If God has blessed your church with lots of children, faithfulness is the greatest gift you can give them! Third John 1:4, "I could have no greater joy than to hear that my children are following the truth" (NLT). This verse should be the goal of every church leadership team, as you pass the baton of faith to future generations.

2. What does a united church leadership team look like?

Respected church leaders are united.

Ephesians 4:3-6, "Make every effort to keep yourselves united in the Spirit, binding yourselves together with peace. For there is one body and one Spirit, just as you have been called to one glorious hope for the future. There is one Lord, one faith, one baptism, one God and Father of all, who is over all, in all, and living through all" (NLT).

Notice that God the Father, Jesus the Lord and Son, and God the Holy Spirit can keep a church united. That is why Jesus prayed to the Father about us in John 17:20-21, "I am praying not only for these disciples but also for all who will ever believe in me through their message. I pray that they will all be one, just as you and I are one—as you are in me, Father, and I am in you" (NLT).

Church leaders, are you listening? Psalm 133:1, "How wonderful and pleasant it is when brothers live together in harmony!" (NLT)

Take risks, be intentional, but make sure that you are a uniter, not a divider.

Ephesians 4:2, "Always be humble and gentle. Be patient with each other, making allowance for each other's faults because of your love" (NLT).

3. What are the essentials to maintaining authentic love in a leadership team?

Respected church leaders are loving.

Jesus said in John 13:35, "Your love for one another will prove to the world that you are my disciples" (NLT).

Church leaders, especially, need to be relentless in their pursuit to love others. First Corinthians 13:7, "Love never gives up, never loses faith, is always hopeful, and endures through every circumstance" (NLT).

The apostle Peter wrote these words to a church under pressure and persecution: 1 Peter 4:8, "Most important of all, continue to show deep love for each other, for love covers a multitude of sins" (NLT).

A Restored, Respected Leadership understands 1 Corinthians 13:13, "Three things will last forever—faith, hope, and love—and the greatest of these is love" (NLT).

In Heaven, there will be no need for faith or hope, but love will last forever!

In May of 1986, my wife and I were sitting in the back of The Worship Center, in an Adult Sunday School Class, at Brownsburg Christian Church (now Connection Pointe Christian Church). We were in a church more than twice the size of Brownsburg Christian, in Cincy. We were a united, loving, and healthy church. We had declined coming to Brownsburg, Indiana, for eight months.

We were thorough in our research, yet very cautious about leaving a caring church of 500 people, in the city where our parents lived. However, as BCC pursued us, The Holy Spirit began to call us.

The church had been deeply wounded for a decade and was on "life support." We finally agreed to preach a "trial sermon," and leave our biological and church family, and move our three preschoolers with us to Brownsburg, Indiana, IF the call from God was clear that May Sunday in 1986.

Frankly, the church resembled an abused spouse. She was the Bride of Christ, but deeply hurt people do not appear to be faithful, united, and loving. They *had* been faithful, were sticking together, and Christ's love was in their DNA ... But when trust has been broken, perseverance and harmony and kindness are not outwardly obvious.

As we sat behind the people in that Sunday School Class, I wondered, "Does God really want me to move my young, comfortable, loved family to this 'damaged' congregation?" But, then, it happened: I looked over at my wife, and she was deeply sobbing. I thought, "OK, Lord. I get it. Some *other* pastor, wife and family with more experience in nursing a twice-split, broken congregation back to health would be better prepared for this task ... To Restore a church with these kinds of scars, a family with older children, would be more qualified to lead this flock and get them back on mission."

Anyway, I preached the "trial sermon." They overwhelmingly voted for us to come, but as soon as we got in our car to head home to Cincy, I apologized. "I'm sorry for dragging you through this grueling process and potentially taking you away from your widowed father and the kind of church that most pastors dream of leading. I will call them when we get home, and tell them we just cannot leave."

To which my bride said, "You don't understand." "I saw you weeping," I said. Then she said, "I can't explain it, but it's as if I *heard The Lord say,* as I looked at those faithful Christian veterans, 'You really are leaving ... your family, your hometown and this church who has shown us what a faithful, united and loving congregation looks like. You have been loved and now I want you to come and just *love these people.*'"

I was speechless, and that doesn't often happen with me. But my wife had heard *His* voice and now I heard Him *through her.*

For the last four decades, I have often heard Him speak to me through her. So ... as we "retire," we have experienced His faithfulness, His Spirit of unity, and His unconditional love through the Parkside Christian Church in Cincinnati, Ohio, and the Connection Pointe Christian Church in central Indiana!

JESUS' SEVENTH PRIORITY: COMMITMENT

The New Testament conveys countless appeals to stand firm, stay strong, and finish well; all encouragements that are intended to produce believers who stand firm in their faith. This should not, however, be interpreted as promoting a static or passive commitment.

Biblical faith must be evident in everyday experiences, the essentials of which Jesus boiled down to two considerations: our relationship with God and the way we treat people. Therefore, one critical way to model commitment is to "remain faithful even when facing death" (Revelation 2:10, NLT).

A somewhat less obvious, yet often more difficult, way for believers to live out a biblical faith is to model a resolute commitment to love, serve, and respect everyone who God puts in their path. This is particularly challenging because human nature is to withhold respect from people who have caused hurt, who appear unworthy, or who do not reciprocate – and there are a lot of them out there.

Consider a family member, even a close family member like a brother or sister, who refuses to show you respect or overtly disrespects you. Think about a parent who attempts to influence you to do something that is contrary to your conscience or desire. Most people would find it very difficult to respond by showing them sincere respect.

But that is precisely Jesus' expectation and it is also the example he set personally. His family members were skeptical of his Messianic identity and role (John 7:5), and His mother prompted Him to perform a miracle before it was His time (John 2:4).

Yet even in the face of those very personal and likely hurtful affronts, Jesus resolved to model love and respect, even to the point that He accounted for His mother's care and provision even while He was hanging on the cross (John 19:26-27). Living out a commitment to show respect is an important way that believers can reflect their Savior and truly live as those who are "called out" as the *Ekklesia*.

CHAPTER EIGHT

RESTORED VICTORY

Since recorded history around 3600 B.C., over 14,500 major wars have killed four billion people …

Most wars are about taking control over territories. But the ultimate war is *over you and me*. In Ephesians, we've learned who God is, what He's done for us and how we should live as a result.

Paul writes: Ephesians 6:10-11, "A final word: Be strong in the Lord and in his mighty power. Put on all of God's armor so that you will be able to stand firm against all strategies of the devil" (NLT).

RESTORING ME

This is a wake-up call! It is hard to stay strong … we get spiritually worn down at times. You have a connection with God … you surrender to Him … you know why you are part of the church and how life should be … But it is difficult. How do you stay on your game?

Paul's final words teach us how to *remain* strong in the Lord. It is more about Who than how.

To keep us relying on the Lord to Restore us, God can use three things as a reminder:

(1) Other people

Have you noticed that no matter how "successful" you are, there are other people who have more, are better, or bigger than you are? People say to me, "Connection Pointe is really an influential church." That's true…but, if I ever start thinking that we've got this church thing figured out, all I have to do is go to a pastors/wives conference … I attended a conference this year with 63 other Christian churches represented. (They averaged in attendance from 1,000 to 25,000. Other people can humble you.)

(2) Past failures (can keep us humble). It's hard to be proud when we remember some of the dumb things we've done.

In the last few years, I lost my balance and did a somersault down the aisle after a wedding…Another time, I started to come out on the platform, and one of our Elders said, "Your zipper is down."

Years ago, I split the seam in my pants just before I rode out on a Harley to introduce a "biker ministry."

When I remember the dumb stuff I've done, it's pretty hard to take yourself too seriously.

And…

(3) Comparison to Christ (will *surely* keep us humble.)

When we see how perfect Jesus was in attitude, Word, and teaching, we can identify with Paul's words in Philippians 3:8-9, "everything else is worthless when compared with the infinite value of knowing Christ Jesus my Lord. For his sake I have discarded everything else, counting it all as garbage, so that I could gain Christ and become one with him. I no longer count on my own righteousness through obeying the law; rather, I become righteous through faith in Christ…" (NLT).

Isaiah 40:28,29,31, "Have you never heard? Have you never understood? The LORD is the everlasting God, the Creator of all the earth. He never grows weak or weary. No one can measure the depths of his understanding. He gives power to the weak and strength to the powerless. … But those who trust in the LORD will find new strength. They will soar high on wings like eagles. They will run and not grow weary. They will walk and not faint" (NLT).

WE ARE AT WAR

However, Restored Victory is about *God.*

GOD IS FOR US

Sometimes we *feel* strong, sometimes we *feel* weak … That is why we need the strength and power of God.

SATAN IS AGAINST US

Ephesians 6:12, "For we are not fighting against flesh-and-blood enemies, but against evil rulers and authorities of the unseen world, against mighty powers in this dark world, and against evil spirits in the heavenly places" (NLT).

In *this* supernatural fight … it's punch, counter punch!

God provides order that gives us peace. Evil destroys peace. God is love. Evil is hatred. God created life. Evil seeks death.

Most surveys say more people believe in God than in Satan. You see much of our world resists the idea of Satan for the same reason people resist believing in God. "We are the masters of the universe!"

So, we are cautioned in 1 Peter 5:8-9, "Stay alert! Watch out for your great enemy, the devil. He prowls around like a roaring lion, looking for someone to devour. Stand firm against him, and be strong in your faith" (NLT).

In the Lord's Prayer, Jesus said we should pray, "*Deliver* us from the evil one."

So … our strength has to come from the Lord. But how?

WE ARE EQUIPPED FOR BATTLE

Ephesians 6:13, "Therefore, put on every piece of God's armor so you will be able to resist the enemy in the time of evil. Then after the battle you will still be standing firm" (NLT).

How *do* we "put on *every piece* of God's armor?"

Ephesians 6:14-17, "Stand your ground, putting on the belt of truth and the body armor of God's righteousness. For shoes, put on the peace that comes from the Good News so that you will be fully prepared. In addition to all of these, hold up the shield of faith to stop the fiery arrows of the devil. Put on salvation as your helmet, and take the sword of the Spirit, which is the word of God" (NLT).

The late Wayne Smith used to tell of a boxer getting beat up every round. He'd drag himself back to the corner. The trainer kept saying, "He hasn't laid a glove on you." (He kept saying that after every round.) Finally, after eleven rounds getting beaten to a pulp, the boxer said, "OK, I'm going back out there, but you keep your eye on the referee, because *somebody's* beatin' the devil out of me!"

Do you know who's beatin' the devil out of you? Not the referee. It's your enemy, Satan.

Sometimes people give us trouble, but they really are not the enemy. Our enemy is not another believer or someone opposed to Christianity.

Here's the truth ... we are at war, and we know who the enemy is (Satan and his demons) ... Here's the good news:

WE WILL WIN

What's the secret to Victory? Ephesians 6:18, "Pray in the Spirit at all times and on every occasion. Stay alert and be persistent in your prayers for all believers everywhere" (NLT).

Prayer is depending on God. Have you ever wondered why it seems so hard to pray? Satan is *resisting* your efforts.

In fact, people often ask, "How can I support you, pastor?" Almost always, I say, "Pray for me." Notice the apostle Paul's words in Ephesians 6:19-20, "Pray for me, too. Ask God to give me the right words so I can boldly explain God's mysterious plan that the Good News is for Jews and Gentiles alike. I am in chains now, still preaching this message as God's ambassador. So pray that I will keep on speaking boldly for him, as I should" (NLT).

Here's God's plan: The more you pray for others, the stronger you and they become spiritually.

RESTORING THE CHURCH

Strength comes from prayer and we exercise strength as we serve!

Matthew 20:26, "Whoever wants to be a leader among you must be your servant..." (NLT).

Galatians 5:13, "For you have been called to live in freedom... But don't use your freedom to satisfy your sinful nature. Instead, use your freedom to serve one another in love" (NLT).

Here are four ways to be strong: "In the Lord and in *His* mighty power."

(1) Be assured: The battle is the Lord's!

When an intimidating army surrounded God's people, the Lord told King Jehosophat, in 2 Chronicles 20:15, "Do not be afraid! Don't be discouraged by this mighty army, for the battle is not yours, but God's" (NLT).

Please don't miss this: We are foolish to engage the enemy or the obstacles, in our strength or power. We stand in the victory Jesus has *already* won when He defeated Satan, at His resurrection! We're like the lion in *The Wizard of Oz* ... "Put 'em up!" We look foolish and he just laughs at us, if *we* think the battle is ours!

Even though we stand in a war zone, we don't *fight* for victory, we live from a *place* of victory.

Colossians 1:13, "For he has rescued us from the kingdom of darkness and transferred us into the Kingdom of his dear Son" (NLT).

Another way to be strong?

(2) Be planted: on solid rock!

Jesus said in Matthew 7:24-25, "Anyone who listens to my teaching and follows it is wise, like a person who builds a house on solid rock. Though the rain comes in torrents and the floodwaters rise and the winds beat against that house, it won't collapse because it is built on bedrock" (NLT).

Our hope is in Christ alone.

Jesus warned that there is a difference between one who "hears" and one who "doesn't obey." When we do obey, it is a supernatural shield against the enemy. But when we choose to disobey, we open ourselves up to a spiritual collapse.

Wanna be strong?

(3) Be fitted: with God's armor.

The armor is God's *supernatural* protection to resist the enemy.

(4) Be strong: in faith!

First Peter 5:9, "Stand firm against him, and be strong in your faith. Remember that your family of believers all over the world is going through the same kind of suffering you are" (NLT).

Don't become a victim ... be victorious! We are not defeated, we are more than conquerors in Jesus! We have all had moments of defeat. But take God at His Word and experience real, lasting victory!

The church is a living organism and it will grow naturally. Leaders have no pressure to make the church grow. We simply must remove the obstacles or weeds, so *Jesus* can build His church.

As a church committed to Restoring the teachings of the New Testament church, God has shown us the model. We glorify Christ by wearing only His name, Christian. Our authority is the Word of the Lord, the Bible. We have no creedal statement but what is taught in the New Testament. We plead for a unity of all God's people upon His Word. Holy living in accordance with the teachings of Jesus Christ and the apostles is necessary to complete our Christianity and make possible eternal life. As God told Moses in Hebrews 8:5, "Be sure that you make everything according to the pattern I have shown you here on the mountain" (NLT).

The plea to *restore* the New Testament Church is an urgent petition to accept the Lordship of Jesus Christ in *all* things in the church. Thomas Campbell said, "The church upon earth is essentially, intentionally and constitutionally *one*." The church is *united* in essence. The church was a deliberate creation of God, not an accidental afterthought of the apostles. The constitutional unity refers to the charter (the Bible) as the express will of the Lord. The rights and privileges in the Scriptures govern the church for all times.

CHARACTERISTICS OF THE CHURCH RESTORED

The church in the Bible recognizes the autonomy of the local congregation

The Church is a simple association of local Christians, meeting around the Lord's table, and worshipping God so people can be connected to Christ and His people. The power of self-government is limited to local or individual congregations. The decision of one congregation applies *only* to that congregation.

In Acts 6:1-6, ministry leaders were chosen from the same congregation for which they were needed: "I left you on the island of Crete so you could complete our work there and appoint elders in each town as I instructed you" (Titus 1:5, NLT). The elders were appointed in every church, not over many churches. The local church did its own disciplining. Jesus said, "Now I say to you that you are Peter (which means 'rock'), and upon this rock I will build my church, and all the powers of hell will not conquer it" (Matthew 16:18, NLT)" – perfect in organization, worship, doctrine, faith and mission.

Ephesians 1:22-23 says, "God has put all things under the authority of Christ and has made him head over all things for the benefit of the church. And the church is his body; it is made full and complete by Christ, who fills all things everywhere with himself" (NLT).

A New Testament Restored Church is governed *locally* and always will be, when we follow the New Testament.

The church in the first century had elders to oversee and shepherd the flock

First Timothy 5:17 reads, "Elders who do their work well should be respected and paid well, especially those who work hard at both preaching and teaching" (NLT). Apparently, the eldership had *one* paid elder "whose work is preaching and teaching" and fellow non-paid elders. They are not just a group of good guys who offer beautiful prayers during communion. Acts 20:28 says: "So guard yourselves and God's people. Feed and shepherd God's flock—his church, purchased with his own blood—over which the Holy Spirit has appointed you as leaders" (NLT). They are to feed, lead, guide and *guard* the church.

Jesus taught the apostles *by example*; the apostles taught the elders *by example*; the elders teach Christians *by example*. The elders' job is not to sort the saints of God; they are to *serve* the saints. We must imitate their faith. With the commandment of Christ behind them and the Spirit of Christ within them, "Remember your leaders who taught you the word of God. Think of all the good that has come from their lives, and follow the example of their faith" (Hebrews 13:7, NLT). After all, the church is the only family some people will ever have. (The elders are responsible to care for us and see that we are fed and do the right things.)

Acts 14:23 says, "Paul and Barnabas also appointed elders in every church. With prayer and fasting, they turned the elders over to the care of the Lord, in whom they had put their trust" (NLT).

The apostle Paul wrote to Titus, the preacher in Crete, in Titus 1:5, "I left you on the island of Crete so you could complete our work there and appoint elders in each town as I instructed you" (NLT).

For church leaders, here are four suggestions on ***appointing elders ...***

(1) *Empower them.*

If someone is qualified to serve as an elder, entrust significant responsibilities to them and *continue* to teach them, after they've learned some things.

Church leaders need to expect that when a church is on fire, smoke *will* get in their eyes! In fact, if you don't want to deal with smoke, don't go to or lead a church to be restored and be on fire!

(2) *Make sure they are on the bus!*

If they are opposed to the church's strategy for being restored and renewed, *do not* appoint them to lead. Ephesians 4:3, "Make every effort to keep yourselves united in the Spirit, binding yourselves together with peace" (NLT).

(3) *Assess the elders every year.*

If someone who is not on board or is "a lid" to progress, it's better to be honest with them than try to talk them into being a united, visionary leader.

(4) *Have a yearly "Blue Sky" retreat.*

Lead them to review the short-term goals, and dream about the long-term.

Ask them to describe the "church of the future," yearly, and the church's vision will remain white hot!

(5) *Don't overlook a Barnabas.*

Some of the best leaders are not as strong on vision, but their gift of encouragement will help the eldership maintain a culture of joy!

The elders and lead pastor are assisted by all the members, who are representatives of the church and are guided by the elders. The blueprint for the church in the Bible always includes a plurality of elders in the local congregation.

The body of Christ observed the Lord's Supper every weekend in remembrance of Christ

Notice Acts 2:42, "All the believers devoted themselves to the apostles' teaching, and to fellowship, and to sharing in meals (including the Lord's Supper), and to prayer" (NLT). And to Acts 20:7, "On the first day of the week, we gathered with the local believers to share in the Lord's Supper. Paul was preaching to them, and since he was leaving the next day, he kept talking until midnight" (NLT). The Bible tells each one to examine himself and then partake. First Corinthians 11:23-30 reads, "For I pass on to you what I received from the Lord himself. On the night when he was betrayed, the Lord Jesus took some bread and gave thanks to God for it. Then he broke it in pieces and said, 'This is my body, which is given for you. Do this in remembrance of me.' In the same way, he took the cup of wine after supper, saying, 'This cup is the new covenant between God and his people—an agreement confirmed with my blood. Do this in remembrance of me as often as you drink it.' For every time you eat this bread and drink this cup, you are announcing the Lord's death until he comes again.

So anyone who eats this bread or drinks this cup of the Lord unworthily is guilty of sinning against the body and blood of the Lord. That is why you should examine yourself before eating the bread and drinking the cup. For if you eat the bread or drink the cup without honoring the body of Christ, you are eating and drinking God's judgment upon yourself. That is why many of you are weak and sick and some have even died" (NLT). Neither is the Lord's Table a re-enactment of the death of Christ – or a mass. We *remember* Him and never forget.

Baptism was by immersion into the body of believers

There is no example of infant baptism found in the Bible. In fact, the term "immersion" is really the word for baptism.

The early Kentucky evangelist, Raccoon John Smith, illustrated this point vividly. At the close of an outdoor baptism, Smith approached a visiting minister and began to pull him toward the water. The minister protested, asking what Smith was doing. Smith replied that he intended to baptize the minister. The minister objected, saying, "Brother Smith, you know if you baptize me against my will it won't do me any good." At that, John Smith stopped and turned to the crowd. "Ladies and gentlemen, last Sunday this man took a little baby and performed for it an act that he termed baptism. And now you have heard from his own lips that it really didn't do any good!" If someone is incapable of faith and incapable of repentance, that person is incapable of being immersed.

Before the apostle Paul was immersed, he was told: "What are you waiting for? Get up and be baptized. Have your sins washed away by calling on the name of the Lord" (Acts 22:16, NLT).

Immersion is a *burial* – do you bury dead or live people? Dead in sin, buried in Christ and then rise to walk in a new kind of life. There is not one verse in the whole Bible that tells you everything you must do to be saved. We are *not* immersed because Jesus was; He is perfect! We are *not* immersed to join a church – *God* adds to His church those who are being saved (Acts 2:47). "And all who have been united with Christ in baptism have put on Christ, like putting on new clothes" (Galatians 3:27, NLT).

A clever jeweler took apart an excellent time piece. He took the various parts and put them in other watches, calling attention to the part of the fine watch in each new watch he made when he made a sale. One man claimed he had the original watch and showed the case as proof of his claim. The next man claimed *he* had the original – he had the face in his watch. Another had the hands, another the main spring, another a diamond jewel. *Each claimed* to have the *original watch.*

Today, many churches point to some particular feature of which they are confident and claim to be the *true* church because of it. They immerse, but regular observance of the Lord's Supper is absent. Deacons are present, but no elders are selected. The church is autonomous, has elders, observes the Lord's Supper regularly, and practices immersion of repenting believers, but righteous living is strangely omitted.

The whole truth is not confined to one or two things, but consists in having *all* that the Lord has authorized in His church. That is the Church Restored!

A FINAL WORD

I encourage you to read our succession plan printed at the end of this book. While this book is not a book on pastoral succession, I *do* want to address the topic because restored churches often lose their momentum because they fail to plan for pastoral succession.

I close this book by reading Paul's final words to the elders of the church in Ephesus: Acts 20:28, "Guard yourselves and God's people. Feed and shepherd God's flock—his church, purchased with his own blood—over which the Holy Spirit has appointed you as leaders" (NLT).

ACTION STEPS FOR OUR STORY

1. *Guard yourself:* (Prayer, the Word of God)

2. *Protect the flock:* (Love them and lead them to follow a God-sized vision.)

3. *Pray for and encourage your leaders.*

We, as works of Restoration in progress, *must* guard our hearts, care for each other, pray for each other, and encourage each other, and God *will* do more than we can ask or imagine!

I write this on October 31, 2017. Five hundred years ago today, an unknown monk in a small village nailed a document to the door of the town church. His name was Martin Luther. His Ninety-Five Theses were a set of theological statements regarding the church of his day.

Luther meant to begin a discussion within the church. However, ecclesiastical authorities eventually condemned him as a heretic. His supporters formed a protest movement calling for reform, leading to the Protestant Reformation.

Just as Martin Luther nailed his Ninety-Five Theses to the door of his church, so Jesus stands at the door of His church today and says, "I stand at the door and knock. If you hear my voice and open the door, I will come in, and we will share a meal together as friends."

"Those who are victorious will sit with me on my throne, just as I was victorious and sat with my Father on His throne.

"Anyone with ears to hear must listen to the Spirit and understand what He is saying to the churches" (Revelation 3:20-22, NLT).

Have and your church opened your door to Jesus?

Take action! Open the door to Jesus! Experience His ongoing work of restoration in you and in your church!

ADDENDUM
PASTORAL SUCCESSION

It is critical for sustaining a restored culture of victory that every church formulates a pastoral succession plan. I have spent the last two years preparing to pass the baton to the next lead minister of the church I've led for the last thirty-one years.

Thinking about the transition, ahead of time, really can make the difference in the legacy succession of the Lord's Church. Unless Jesus returns, a pastoral succession is inevitable.

Three components must be considered:

Emergency Succession

Regardless of the age of the pastor, church leaders owe it to the congregation to write an emergency plan. That's because, in addition to an unexpected death, there are many potential emergency scenarios: moral failure, church splits, a pastor's theological shift, financial scandal, and other "messy" situations.

The Vanderbloemen Search Group, a church staffing company, says one in every four churches that comes to them for pastoral succession assistance is dealing with an unexpected end to their pastor's ministry. So developing an emergency succession plan is Job One.

An emergency succession plan (or ESP) should include the name of the new interim day-to-day leader and clearly stated areas of responsibility. To whom will this leader be accountable? What decisions is the interim leader prohibited from making without approval of the governing board? (For example: firing and hiring staff, changes to financial practices).

The governing board, or elders, should also state the term of the new day-to-day leader, given the specific circumstances at the time. The board should establish the process and timing of the naming of the new lead pastor, according to the church's existing governing documents, and announce this process no later than ninety days after the appointment of the new day-to-day leader.

In the case of serious illness, the current lead pastor and the governing board should mutually decide when the lead pastor will reassume his role.

The ESP should be signed by the current lead pastor and the chair of the governing board.

Caution: In my opinion, this information should be known only by the chair and one other person, and filed in a confidential place, known only by those two church members. (Public dialogue surrounding this plan opens up all kinds of potentially divisive issues.)

In our case, I have also recommended interim weekend speakers, who would NOT be candidates for the new lead pastor role. This ensures that the day-to-day leader can focus on daily operations, while a seasoned, gifted Bible teacher can provide "fresh bread" for the congregation on the weekends. This is especially important in a transition time when the truth and comfort of God's Word can unite and strengthen the body.

The Transition

The key to developing a successful succession plan is to ask the right questions and truthfully answer them, based on your current reality.

Here are some key questions:

- What will the lead pastor do *after* the transition? Should the pastor still be a part of the church family, depart for a mutually agreed upon time, or leave the church family permanently? If the former pastor stays or returns to the church family, what boundaries need to be clarified regarding his role?

- What goals would the current lead pastor like to accomplish between now and the transition?

- What boundaries need to be clarified regarding the role of the former lead pastor's wife, if they stay or return to be a part of the congregation?

- Who should be included in developing and carrying out the succession plan?

- What is the anticipated date of retirement?

- What can the church do to help ensure the lead pastor's financial needs are adequately provided for after he leaves?

- Who will be on the new pastor search team?

- How long should the new pastoral candidate work with the current lead pastor, if that is a part of the succession plan?

- What two primary strengths should the next lead pastor have?

- When the lead pastor retires, who (meaning the elders, staff, congregation) needs to know what and when?

- What is the ideal size of the group to be involved in the details of a transition plan? Should there be more than one group (one to review candidates, one to plan communications and outreach to the congregation, etc.)?

- Is a template available for identifying and estimating transition costs that would be helpful to the church?

Three Years After the Transition

Our succession plan team also found it helpful to anticipate what a successful succession plan would look like three years *after* it takes place.

This included the outgoing lead pastor and spouse, the incoming lead pastor and spouse, the congregation, the church staff, the senior leadership/board/elders, and the surrounding community.

In our case, the vision of a successful succession, plus three years, is a congregation that is still thriving and united.

The former lead pastor and spouse are in a good place financially, relationally, and spiritually. The incoming pastor and spouse have been warmly embraced by the leadership, staff, and the congregation. More and better disciples are being transformed. The congregation is healthy financially, and continues to be generous with our community and global partners.

Here's the truth: Even in the healthiest church, there will be grief. Relationships will change. Not every member of the congregation, nor even every leader, will embrace the transition.

But that does not change the *responsibility* of the pastor and leadership of the church to transition when it is time. Together they must navigate the waters of succession in a spirit of grace, truth, and unity.

Six weeks after my last weekend, I returned to introduce my successor to the congregation. There were just over 5,000 in attendance! That's a pretty good start on Connection Pointe's pastoral succession, and for that I am grateful!

ABOUT THE AUTHOR

STEVE REEVES retired from 40 years of pastoral ministry in October 2017. He served as Lead Pastor at Connection Pointe Christian Church in Brownsburg, Indiana, for over 31 years. The church, which relocated to a 118-acre site in November of 2001, grew from 250 to an average weekly attendance of 4,200 during his 31 years as Lead Pastor. A recent campus expansion added a children's building that accommodates up to 600 children per service, an expanded front lobby space, a new 500-seat adult worship venue, renovation of existing space into a student worship venue seating 300, as well as 13 small group breakout rooms for students, and the existing worship center was expanded to seat 1,200.

Steve is now serving as the Engage Pastor with Leadership Network, where he will come alongside pastors of churches with primarily over 2,000 attendance. He is also on the Advisory Board and is a Consultant for The Center for Church Leadership, which offers coaching and resources to enhance the ministry of primarily smaller non-denominational "Christian" churches.

Steve graduated from Cincinnati Bible College and attended Cincinnati Christian Seminary. He is a past member of the NACC Board of Stewards (Treasurer and Chairman of the Board 1998 – 2001). He served as a Regional Vice-President of the 2005 NACC. Steve and his wife, Kristen, have been married 41 years and have three grown children and three grandchildren.